Henry Briscoe's warm word ... the many simple but important lessons of life we tend to forget. "Hank" was a good man—be sure to read and reread his article *What is a Good Man?*
– *William V. McBride,*
General, USAF (Retired)

Brush Country Bull is a delightfully humorous collection of Henry's columns sure to cause many to laugh and others to reminisce about the "good ol' days" of growing up in rural Texas.
– *Bill Dean, Executive Vice President,*
Texas Tech Alumni Association

With a sharp eye for detail and an appreciation for simple pleasures, Henry Briscoe has crafted short, pungent pieces that evoke a time when you could go to town, leave your truck unlocked, and return to find your tools and gun still on the front seat; a time when "dining out" meant eating your dinner next to a hay baler, and when "entertainment" for teenagers consisted of a dip in a muddy swimming hole in the company of snakes and turtles. Laced with humor and the occasional provocative political barb, *Brush Country Bull* is a testament to a particular time and place, and to the skills of its deft chronicler.
– *Jackie Jones, University of Texas*

Henry Briscoe, Texan to the core, delights his readers—especially those who love Texas history—with saucy tales and frontier wit. To miss any of Henry's articles would be like stopping in the middle of a Larry McMurtry book.
– *The Medina County Historic Commission*

Brush Country Bull

Observations of a South Texas
Sportsman, Historian, Pilot,
and Patriot

Brush Country Bull

Observations of a South Texas Sportsman, Historian, Pilot, and Patriot

Volume I
1977-1980

Henry B. Briscoe

WESTBOW
PRESS

WestBow Press books may be ordered through booksellers or by contacting:

WestBow Press
A Division of Thomas Nelson
1663 Liberty Drive
Bloomington, IN 47403
www.westbowpress.com
1-(866) 928-1240

Because of the dynamic nature of the Internet, any web addresses or links contained in this book may have changed since publication and may no longer be valid. The views expressed in this work are solely those of the author and do not necessarily reflect the views of the publisher, and the publisher hereby disclaims any responsibility for them.

Any people depicted in stock imagery provided by Thinkstock are models, and such images are being used for illustrative purposes only.

Certain stock imagery © Thinkstock.

ISBN: 978-1-4497-3944-7 (sc)
ISBN: 978-1-4497-3945-4 (hc)
ISBN: 978-1-4497-3943-0 (e)

Library of Congress Control Number: 2012901998

Printed in the United States of America

WestBow Press rev. date: 3/7/2012

To everything there is a season,

       and time to every purpose

              under the heavens;

A time to keep silence

       And a time to speak . . .

             Ecclesiastes 3:1

ACKNOWLEDGEMENTS

So many faithful friends and family members have contributed their expertise, time and energy to this project. I want to express my deep gratitude for their input, encouragement, and support of this project. My list begins with the Dubose family of *The Devine News* (especially KK Dubose Calame, the current publisher and owner) who ran Henry's articles for 27 years. Driscoll Public Librarian Barbara Moore was an invaluable help with the microfiche machine as we researched and verified publication dates for each article. Frances Lawson provided invaluable computer expertise when we needed to extract and copy Henry's files from his computer after his death. Adeline Bohl, who grew up with Henry, spent many hours alongside me at the microfiche machine, copying Henry's articles. The project simply would not have gotten off the ground without the enthusiasm and encouragement of The Medina County Historical Society. And we're so grateful to the editors and project managers at Westbow Press for their endless patience and guidance. But this was also a family project. Our daughters Marianne Outlaw and Sue Stewart worked on data entry and editing, while our grandchildren Emalee Smith and Colby Stewart also helped with data entry. Daughter Kate Eastburn and Julie Mize, an in-law, helped with proofreading. Mark Stewart, our son-in-law, designed the book cover, and our son Ben Briscoe offered me cheerful assistance and never-failing problem solving.

I am also most grateful for the many loyal readers of *Brush Country Bull* who "couldn't wait for next week's paper to hit the streets."

Mary B. Briscoe

To the readers
who find within these pages
a companion

CONTENTS

1979

Introduction

L-R: Henry Briscoe, Nancy Briscoe McAnelly, G.H. Briscoe.

In 1931, a barefoot, tow-headed 5-yr-old milked cows, rode a paint pony bareback, and sat with his family on the front porch on summer evenings. If he thought about the future at all, he probably saw a larger version of himself milking cows, chasing ponies and sitting with his own family on the front porch. Flying airplanes to Guam or Khartoum, taking accounting classes in college or serving as a Medina County commissioner would have all been inconceivable life scenarios to young Henry Briscoe. Even more improbable would have been a long-running journalism career. He had notoriously bad handwriting and chided himself about his less-than-stellar performance in school. And yet, each of these professional eventualities found him—drawn by his enthusiasm, his strong work ethic balanced by a jovial spirit, and a sense of humility and gratitude. We often heard him say, "I don't know why God has given me such a great life."

Like most optimists, Henry's interests were widely varied. Even as a boy, his sponge-like mind soaked up the smallest details of his country environment near Devine, Texas. His years in the Air Force multiplied those interests as he flew around the world and served in Vietnam and the Pentagon. So in one sense, it might have seemed coincidental when, after retiring to his boyhood home from the Air Force, several of his articles about a deer-hunting contest in *The Devine News* morphed into a weekly column. But in another sense it was inevitable. It would take 27 years to download all the experiences, images, details and opinions he had collected over the years into the weekly column known as Brush Country Bull. And over the years, he sharpened his "tools" for developing a subject: keen observations, an avid interest, common sense, personal experience, and in many cases, a search for truth.

He wrote often about his first love—the Brush Country itself. It had his heart and like a dear friend, he paid very close attention to it. He cared for it, hunted in it, and marveled at its dangers and beauties. His love for America was a natural outgrowth of that first love, intensified by his years in the military. At every mealtime blessing, he asked God to protect "our great nation." Still, he was a realist and could rail with the best of 'em about what wasn't going right in Washington. When it reached the diatribe stage, he could sound like a redneck bigot. He'd always laugh when we called him on it and of course, he'd "stifle" himself a bit. But he stood strong on foundational American ideals and when attacks on those ideals were tolerated, he swung into action—which mostly took the form of language, be it articles, letters to the editor, or talks to various groups. "What's tolerated today will be accepted tomorrow!" was a recurring theme. But even those who disagreed with him could see that his strong political opinions were rooted in an untainted desire for this nation's good. Although he was known to recant a conclusion or statement that had been proven erroneous, once he had "studied out" an issue, he stood by it. His deep reverence for the First Amendment to the Constitution was only equaled by his reverence for the Second. He championed and practiced both tirelessly.

We have so many happy memories of this countrified Renaissance man who was such a good husband and father, but a favorite is of countless Sunday afternoons when we could hear him at the typewriter, pounding out a political concern or transported back to some Indian battle or childhood tale. As objectively as possible, we can affirm that Henry Briscoe's memories and musings have a timeless quality about them. The heart of his philosophical and political principles still ring true today because he relied on a rare combination of common sense, accuracy of perception, persistence— and above all, a ready humor and unaffected love of life.

In remembrance—

Mary B. Briscoe
Sue Briscoe Stewart
Kate Briscoe Eastburn
Ben T. Briscoe
Marianne Briscoe Outlaw

L-R: Ben Briscoe, Marianne Briscoe Outlaw, Kate Briscoe Eastburn, Sue Briscoe Stewart, Mary B., Henry.

BRUSH COUNTRY BULL 1977

Messing with Nature: Risky Business

In the farm and ranch section of a nearby large city newspaper, there recently appeared a very short advertisement: "Lion cub, very gentle and loveable—$750." Now, I really don't understand what a lion cub has to do with farm and ranch operations, but just in case someone has ideas about acquiring that cub, there are a couple of points one ought to ponder before forking over the $750. Unfortunately for the owner, that loveable cub will not remain loveable forever. Second, it absolutely will not remain a cub forever, and as it grows, so will its appetite. Have you ever stopped to think what might be the intake for an adult lion? An adult tiger will kill and eat forty-three medium-to-large animals in a year with a gross intake of about 7,600 pounds. I imagine an adult lion would eat a similar amount. For you folks who don't have an extra 7,600 pounds of meat, I might suggest something smaller for a pet—say a guinea pig or parakeet.

As I was thinking about this situation, it occurred to me that I haven't seen many bobcats around lately. Although the bobcat's appetite isn't as great as the lion's, both animals are carnivorous. I imagine that the bobcat preys on smaller animals, including rabbits, field mice, ground squirrels, and possibly the young of small domestic animals, such as goats, sheep, and hogs. With the tremendous price now being paid for the bobcat's pelt, I wonder if it isn't going to become even more endangered. Some would say, "Good riddance, and well done. We need to get shed of that critter, anyway." Personally, I don't see it that way. I like to see those ol' cats, and I like to know they're around. I also like to know there are a few mountain lions, cougars, and panthers out there in the brush, too. It's exciting to see and talk about seeing one of these cats; experiencing something like that makes our lives more interesting. "But them boogers [cats] kill my calves, lambs, etc." If that is the case, government trappers ought to be alerted to track down the specific culprit, but we shouldn't declare wholesale war on the entire cat population. Some states, like California, have declared the mountain lion an endangered species. If the cats are becoming endangered, then other states should take similar action.

Before this country was settled, the mountain lion served as a check and balance on the deer population, just as the coyote does for jackrabbits. With the many hunters today, we no longer need the mountain lion to control the deer population. But since we no longer "need" him, is that justification to exterminate a species? I say no way—and that goes for any critter. I sincerely hope our state game department is watching the population density of these animals, particularly in view of the high price paid for the bobcat's pelt, so that we don't do with them what our forefathers did with other members of the animal kingdom.

Chicken Hawks and Leghorns

East of Devine in the '30s, '40s, and '50s, one of my mother's many family responsibilities was to tend a flock of chickens. In those days, few farmers had chickens confined to a pen—mostly ours just ran loose and fended for themselves. For many years, Mom's chickens were white leghorns. Now, there are definite disadvantages in having white leghorns that run loose. First, a white leghorn is a rather small bird, about eatin' size for a large hawk, and second, they're a little conspicuous. An alert hawk with average eyesight that's cruising over Lytle at a thousand feet on a clear day can easily zero in on a juicy, unsuspecting white leghorn that's scratching around on a farm east of Devine. And in those days, they sometimes did.

Our ol' leghorns established an alert signal, and when one would observe a large bird overhead, it'd give out with a kind of long, squawking sound. It seemed to me that they'd try to give the signal so that Mom could hear it. When the signal was given, the perceptive and intelligent leghorns would rush headlong for the garage, a shed, a bush, or any available shelter. Mom would dash for the back porch, grab an old Remington rolling block, a single-shot .22, and a handful of "shorts." In the early part of World War II, when airplanes really began a heavy flying schedule in this area, the ol' leghorns sometimes had difficulty discerning the difference between a chicken hawk and, say, a P-40. Happily, Mom never shot down any friendly aircraft before the old cluckers learned that "iron birds" were no threat.

Well, anyway, sometimes there'd be a young pullet that hadn't learned the alert signal, and the ol' hawk would make its kill. By the time Mom had collected her artillery, the hawk would be enjoying its meal on a favorite perch, a large fence post about 150 yards behind the barn. Now, Mom could do most anything well, but here was one thing she couldn't do worth a flip: shoot. She'd load that ol' .22 and shoot in a northerly direction, since that was where the hawk and the remnants of her pullet were situated. As I said, Mom's shootin' wasn't too accurate, and to make matters worse, every time she'd shoot, that old hawk would flap its wings just once, as if to say, "Ha, you missed me again." That would cause Mom's temperature to rise. She'd start shooting a little faster. Finally, she would get within range, and dust would fly within fifteen or twenty yards of the hawk. Then the hawk would leisurely pick up the pullet's remains and fly off to finish eating in a place that provided a little more hospitality.

Mom had an intense dislike for chicken hawks, and she would be disappointed to know that her son now advocates that hunters and shooters treat hawks as friends. Mostly, hawks help far more than they hurt. Basically, they help control the field mice population, which could get out of hand if we didn't have hawks. So the next time you see an ol' hawk sitting out there on top of a dead mesquite and you have your "pickup gun" along, don't shoot unless it happens to be eating a white leghorn. Then it might be prudent to help our poultry men—and Mom would be happy you did.

Man and Beast

O ne of the more interesting aspects of life, I believe, is the relationship that exists between human beings and members of the animal kingdom. Sometimes those relationships can be very close, as between a rodeo performer and his horse or a circus trainer and his animals. Under normal circumstances, people certainly form some sort of impression about almost any animal when they are in frequent contact with that animal. Anyone who has had much contact with animals will learn early that animals, too, are individuals and have their own personal characteristics and traits that differ from other animals of the same species.

When I was a child, my father operated a dairy at a time when milking machines could only be found at the far end of one's arm. It didn't take long for me to learn that each one of those cows had a different sort of attitude about things. Our milking assignments were allocated so that the kids milked the contented cows and Dad took on those with apparent chronic ulcers and mean dispositions. The meanest cow of all was Ol' Lightning, a black cow that wasn't either Holstein or Jersey. Lightning was given that name not because of her great speed across the countryside but because she could kick ya off the milking stool and then get ya three more times before ya hit the ground. She was fast with those rear feet, and when she really got upset, she'd come off the ground with both hind legs simultaneously. You'd better be quick, because she'd ruin your entire day. Anyway, needless to say, a sort of relationship developed between Dad and Lightning. Each saw the other as a challenge. Twice a day, during her milk-giving times, the battle raged. His attitude was, "I'm gonna get that milk," and hers was, "No, you ain't." The result was that Dad would get some milk, Lightning would "hold some up," and usually the cats got the most after she'd kicked both Dad and the bucket over. Well, fortunately, Dad had only one Lightning. This is but one of many relationships I've observed between humans and animal—a relationship illustrating, among other things, the individuality of animals.

Certainly the same sort of individuality exists in wildlife. Last winter, I developed a close understanding with a small buck, about three points. We called him Dumbo. He was absolutely beautiful, and we began to first see him before the season opened when we were feeding corn. Almost every evening Dumbo would be waiting for his supper. Sometimes you could walk within forty yards, pour out the corn, and Dumbo would never move a muscle except to turn his head and watch your every move. Sometimes he would be looking over a pear bush, sometimes behind a mesquite, and sometimes he'd be right out in the open. Even if Dumbo had had a large rack, I couldn't have pulled the trigger because, you see, over the weeks, some sort of mutual understanding developed. If I'd shot, I would have "broken the faith." So there's another kind of relationship, and I'm sure there are millions of wonderful and mysterious cases like that between man and beast.

Making the Most of Deer Blind Time

Ya know, hunters can spend a lot of time just sittin' and waitin' in a deer blind. In the morning hunt, ya get there before daylight and leave about nine-thirty or so, and then in the afternoon hunt, ya spend another three hours. Whatta ya do all that time? Daydream? Doze? Whittle? If it's on a Saturday or Sunday afternoon, some might have a portable radio or TV and tune in on the football game using an earpiece. But mostly I suspect the average hunter sits, listens, looks, and thinks.

Why not use that time to improve your knowledge of the outdoors? One way you can start is by learning a little more about the birds that inhabit Brush Country. Usually there are plenty of birds around—and if there aren't, you'd best move your blind, because you may be in a "dead spot." Not only will there be no birds, but they'll also be no rabbits, coyotes, or deer. There are places like that. Anyway, "birding" is an interesting pastime, and as you become more involved, you can recognize them not only by sight, but also by calls and migration patterns. The best way to begin birding is by obtaining a good book such as *Birds of North America* by Robbins, Bruun, Zim, and Singer, published by the Golden Press. Get that or a similar book and take it to the blind with you. When one of our feathered friends flies by and you don't recognize it, look it up. If it is early in the deer season, it might be a Cactus Wren—a giant as far as wrens go.

How many times do you look up and see an ol' buzzard floating by? Did you know there are two kinds—the ol' Turkey Vulture, and then there's a Black Vulture? Both are black, but the Black Vulture has a black head and white wingtips and flies with a more rapid wing beat.

Well, when you get all checked out on the Brush Country bird population, don't quit there. There are similar books on wildflowers, trees, rocks, reptiles, insects, and wild animals. So, go ahead and get ready now for next hunting season. Get your bookshelves built in the blind and your card index system established, and you'll be ready, regardless of what comes by. Then the next time you have your little son, daughter, grandson, or granddaughter out and they say, "Hey Pa, what's that?" you can say, "Well now, there's a Zenaidura Macroura," or Mourning Dove.

Finally, when you're in the blind reading, don't forget to look out every now and then. If ya see that ol' buck and move too quickly to pick up your wild animal book, you can probably determine pretty quickly that he's a White Tail, because that's all you'll see as he takes off through the brush.

The Next Best Thing in Deer Blinds

If ya haven't been too successful hunting for that ol' buck in recent seasons, the reason may be that you're hunting from an outdated blind. Only those who are "out of it" would hunt from a square or rectangular deer blind. The "in" crowd will hunt from a pyramid-shaped blind this year—because, you see, the pyramid is the answer for whatever ails you.

As examples—should you have a long-time, rare, tropical foot fungus, simply sitting in a pyramid blind will cure you—*presto,* just like that. Same goes for an eye twitch, freckles, toothache—no matter. You'll be cured. Not only that, but after sitting there for a while, your vision will improve, your hearing will be more keen, and you'll even be able to smell that ol' buck before he can smell you. Better yet, you'll be able to sense when the buck is sneaking through the woods and might be able to accurately predict his size and the number of points. If you sit there for more than two hours, forget the gun. You won't need it. When the ol' buck shows, if you're younger than eighty-five, you can simply run him down and just let him have a moderate karate chop between the horns. That'll take care of it. Just pitch him over your shoulder, and trot on in to camp.

Well, ya can't just go out and build any ol' pyramid blind. The dimensions must be proper, otherwise it won't work just right. If you'd like one about six feet high, you'll need a base that's exactly 9.4248 feet square, and each upright triangular side would be 8.9647 feet. When ya get the thing built and are ready to put it where ya want it, don't just drop it there. It has to be oriented with the cardinal points of the compass. There are also a number of other precautions in properly placing your pyramid blind. Don't ever put it over some prickly pear, because if ya do, that cactus will start growing right before your eyes. It might just get you before you can get outta there. Also, don't ever put it up in a mesquite tree. That ol' buck might walk under it and possibly end up smarter than you!

Anyway, when you get it built to the proper specs and aligned with the cardinal compass points, then—and only then—will you be ready to receive the cosmic orchestration that embraces the whole celestial universal nebulae. After doing all this, if the cosmic orchestration isn't such that it gives you the hunting success you desire, don't blame me. I really didn't say I advocate the pyramid blind; I simply wanted you to know about it so you'd have sufficient time to get your blind replaced, as hundreds of others will be doing. It's nothing but a courtesy alert that in the deer blind world, anyway, "there may be a change in the shape of things to come."

Sanctuary

The one factor that most threatens our wildlife is the loss of its habitat. Man converts millions of acres annually from the raw state to fields for crops to feed the ever-increasing world populations, airports for transporting these new folks, and highways. Finally, housing developers subdivide large acreages into thousands of smaller plots. Some of our fauna have been able to cope with the increased encroachment of mankind, like the coyote, whitetail deer, armadillo, and others. But most haven't fared too well, such as the grizzly bear, wolf, cougar, and buffalo.

Anybody can turn a backyard into a wildlife paradise if he or she is willing to spend a few cents a day and just a small amount of time. For that small investment in time and money, you can have a tremendous amount of entertainment. When my family lived in Alexandria, Virginia, we had a family of seven squirrels and an untold number of birds on the patio daily. Most of the squirrels learned to eat from your hand, and one would come in the house, climb on your lap, take a peanut, and scamper outside to eat it. Many times I would be reading on the patio and feel the wet touch of a squirrel's nose on my feet. It was always Grey Squirrel who didn't know the difference between a person's foot and hand but thought a peanut should be in either. So if you put out feed, you may not have doves, quail, and deer on a city lot, but you'll have a yard full of birds of all kinds and may attract a squirrel or two. It's an interesting and entertaining pastime for you and the kids and will provide a small sanctuary for our vanishing wildlife.

Taking a Stand on Private Gun Ownership

If I had to name the one material factor which has contributed the most in our being able to celebrate America's 201st anniversary last Monday, I'd say that factor was private gun ownership. Without that one element, the Pilgrims could not have sustained their shaky beginning, and there could have been no successful revolution giving this great nation its start. There would have been no push westward, and Texas—and all of the Southwest, for that matter—would probably still belong to Mexico. Without private gun ownership, there would be no America as we know it.

In spite of that heritage, there are people today in America—dedicated people—who are devoting their untiring energy and efforts toward restricting our right to private ownership of firearms. And that is a real burr in my craw. It cuts to the quick. You see, these well-meaning folks believe, to some extent, that if there were no guns, there would be fewer murders and robberies, hence less crime. Guns, they say, are the problem. Evidence, facts, experience, etc. are not important to these folks; they operate and thrive on notions and ideas. They say we need more rules and regulations—gun control, in a word.

Never mind that Washington, DC has the most stringent gun control laws known to mankind. So the capital city's crime rate is the lowest in the nation, right? Wrong. For some reason, a criminal doesn't pay much attention to the law. Laws are made for others. So just because it's illegal to possess a weapon, it doesn't mean that criminals are going to turn in their weapons lock, stock, and barrel. In Switzerland, practically every adult is issued a weapon as part of that nation's self-defense force. Switzerland has one of the world's lowest crime rates. So from those two situations, one might conclude that private gun ownership and availability of guns has little to do with a nation's crime rate. A high crime rate, in my opinion, is due mostly to an apathetic citizenry—apathetic in that the judicial system has far too many lenient judges and a parole system which, in short order, will release a "rehabilitated" incorrigible to prey on good, honest, taxpaying American citizens. Swift and sure justice is the one way to curb a soaring crime rate. In other words, take the incorrigibles off the streets.

I don't—and I know most of you don't—want to lose the right to private gun ownership. The few guns I have aren't valuable; they're just my old shootin' irons. But I love these old guns. I like the appearance of an ol' Model 94 Winchester and all of the old Winchester lever actions. I like the way they feel. There's nothing like the sound of a solid bolt action rifle such as the Model 70 Winchester or a Model 700 Remington when ya ram that ol' bolt home. And late in the afternoon, when there's no wind, ya let fly with one of those long, long shots with a big bore and listen to the echo (to the echo, to the echo …). There's nothing like it. And there's nothing wrong with it. So let's press on, gun owners, and mix it with the anti-gun, anti-hunting groups. Again, the way you can be most effective is by joining the National Rifle Association and supporting their Institute for Legislative Action. You'll be glad you did.

Wisdom Teeth and Pheasant Hunting

Today is D-Day—that's Dove Day—and if ya happen to live in the southeastern part of Medina county, you're probably wondering where all the doves are. The answer to that question is: they're in the South Zone. Our game department long ago divided Texas into North and South Zones, and in this area, we're just about on the dividing line. Because the state has been divided in this fashion for so long, the doves have long since run that data through their computers and learned that on September 1, it's healthier to reside in the South Zone. So they head just across the county line and set up camp until about September 24; by that time, hunters will converge on the South Zone, and the doves will drift back across into the North Zone, where everyone "knows" there are no doves. Doves are like that.

Anyway, the Lord willin', I'll be out after 'em bright and early this morning—but there was a time in my life when I could never be certain where opening morning of dove season would find me. Most of my younger adult years were spent as a transport pilot in the Military Airlift Command. On any given opening day of dove season, I might be in Japan, Europe, Africa, or almost any place. But pheasant season was something else. As much as I love dove hunting, I like to hunt pheasant even more. So when living in Moses Lake, Washington, I worked out a scheme whereby I'd be present for every opening day of pheasant season, and it wasn't that tough to do. I tried to avoid the "gold brick" label, and when it came my time to fly, I flew birthdays, holidays, anniversaries, no matter—but pheasant season was different.

Ya see, Uncle Sam is kinda partial to keeping his crews and aircraft safe, so if a pilot just happens to be on some sort of strong medication, he's grounded—can't fly. The problem is, how does one schedule medication? Simple—there weren't too many dentists around the Air Force in those days—or now either, for that matter—and when you had a dental appointment, you kept it. So I was fortunate enough to arrive on scenic Moses Lake with four wisdom teeth—spares. I didn't need any of them, and at times, they gave me problems. And if ya want to go pheasant hunting on opening morning and you're apt to be flying in some far-off place, ya simply schedule the removal of just one wisdom tooth about twenty-four hours before opening morning—and *presto*, when they give ya that pain preventative injection, you're grounded for forty-eight hours. That worked perfectly. I had four wisdom teeth and stayed there for four years and never missed an opening day. Had I been there any longer—well …

HB in Korea, 1954.

So regardless of what excuses you have to use or what diversionary tactic you have to pull in order to go hunting this morning, I hope you find a few ol' dumb doves in the North Zone and that ya hit at least 15 percent of your shots. Also, don't litter, follow all the rules, be considerate, and have an all-around great Opening Day.

Hunters: Beware of Circadian Rhythms

Circadian rhythm is a term not too many Brush Country folks would have cause to know about except possibly those who've traveled extensively in modern intercontinental aircraft. As I understand it, circadian rhythm has to do with the internal involuntary "computers" everyone has which help us to go about our daily routine in more or less a timely fashion. For example, most of us really don't need an alarm clock. We've been waking at a certain time each morning for years, and the reason we do that is because our total system is geared to that schedule; after a time, we're "locked in." Sometimes we'd just as soon that system didn't work so well, because we'd like to sleep, say, past 5:30 a.m. on Saturdays and Sundays. Anyway, if one travels around the world, you can forget about a normal circadian rhythm, because as you start going from one time zone to another, it takes days to adjust. You can imagine what happens to one's circadian rhythm when you take off from an East Coast location at 7:00 on a Wednesday morning; stop at Anchorage, Alaska for fuel; and then go on to Tokyo about seven hours later on Thursday evening. For you, the sun has never gone down—and worse, some twenty hours would have elapsed since your last sleep. This is when you're dog-tired and would have something to eat and hit the sack. In about two hours, your internal clock would say, "Hey, Dad, it's time to get up"—terrible.

Anyway, there are other factors that sometimes disrupt our rhythm; therefore, alarm clocks may still be a good buy to assure we wake up at the proper time. A few years back, a Devine resident—an outdoorsman type—loaded up his equipment and a young son and headed for deer country. They arrived kinda late, set up the tent, had a hasty meal, rolled out the sleeping gear, and hit the hay. No need to set the alarm clock—you see, this young fella had been getting up early every morning for years, and his circadian rhythm was "on time." Well, sure enough, it worked again, and ol' Dad got the bacon and eggs going while Junior was dressing. They finished breakfast, shouldered their muskets, and headed for the blind. Since the younger member of this twosome was very young, they both occupied the same blind. The pair turned their attention to the east and kept watching for the faint glow of dawn. Time dragged, stood still, but nothing happened. The sun flat wasn't going to appear that morning.

Ol' Dad had not brought his watch on that trip, and the alarm clock was back in camp, so they really didn't know the time. After eons and eons, they bailed outta the blind and headed for camp, marched into the tent, and retrieved the clock. Let's see, the little hand was at two, and the big hand was at twelve. Ol' Dad (aka George Redus) had a subconscious circadian rhythm breakdown that sort of interrupted the sweet hours of sleep. But no matter. George made up for the lost sleep later when the sun came up and he was sittin' in the blind … snoozing.

Jackrabbits and Black Jacks

As I said in an earlier article, in the "good ol' days," things weren't so good. And that included firearms. I wasn't alone in that my shooting iron lacked in quality. In the forties, my father always had a few winter oat patches and so did some of the neighbors. Also in those days, jackrabbits were numerous. A good source of evening entertainment was to load up my old Model A Ford roadster with a few buddies and their shootin' irons and head for the oat patches to try and reduce the number of those pesky critters.

I can well remember some of the shootin' irons we had on one of those forays. For that kind of shooting, I usually relied on my father's old double barrel 12 gauge—the one that broke in two on practically every shot and threw both shells back in my eyes. Then this one clown had his favorite weapon, a snub-nosed .32 caliber revolver. He could put all of them shots in a fifteen-foot diameter circle at 15 feet but could do no better. Obviously he was no threat to the ol' jackrabbits. Slue had his .22 bolt action single shot. His rate of fire was about three rounds every five minutes, because besides the fact that the trigger guard was bent, the thing would seldom extract an empty hull. Then there was this other dude with a .410 Harrington and Richardson single shot (1902 vintage) with a rusty, worn-out firing pin which would fire once out of every five times ya pulled the trigger. Finally, one of our party was somewhat better equipped. His was also a .22 bolt-action single shot, but it was fairly new. The problem was, his shooting was terrible.

With that kind of offensive array, one can plainly see there was absolutely no threat to the jackrabbit population. After dark, we'd pull into one of those fields in that ol' Model A, strike a match to see if the headlights were on, and then set sail. In the dim lights, one could see these grey, ghostlike forms hurtling every direction as the firing commenced, with two shooters in the rumble seat, two and a half in the front, and no one hitting anything. This one time, we chased all the rabbits outta the oat patches and headed east for the blackjacks. Down there, we ran into this ol' jack, so our radar locked in on him, and we trailed him for what seemed like hours in and out of the trees. We fired all of our ammo, and the ol' jack was unscathed. Finally, from fatigue and probably malnutrition, the ol' jack kinda leaned up against a jack oak to catch his breath. The sportsman guy with the good gun bailed outta the rumble seat, and as he closed on the restin' rabbit, he said something like, "I'll get that devil!" He seized his .22 by the end of the barrel and took this horrendous "Casey at the bat" swing. The ol' rabbit kinda ducked, and you guessed it—the air was filled with splinters as the rifle stock shattered against the more stable blackjack oak.

The ol' rabbit mustered a little strength and half-trotted off while the sportsman crept back to the Model A, cradling what was left of his once-proud musket in one arm and holding four numb fingers of his other hand in his mouth. That moment closed the book on another thrilling jackrabbit expedition in the good ol' days. Score? Jackrabbits: 1; Sportsmen: 0.

OCTOBER 27, 1977

Enthusiasm and Harmless Exaggeration

Ya know, the next best thing to hunting is talking about it, and for those of you who are new to Brush Country, you want to be kinda alert to what is being said, because sometimes some Brush Country hunters get a little excited and might kinda skew their facts a tad. The longer some of these folks talk, the more twisted the facts can become.

One guy who was well-known around this area told me that he read something about bucks needing a lot of protein to produce a large set of antlers. So he rushed out and bought some high-protein deer feed blocks, built what he thought were cow-proof but not deer-proof pens at a number of strategic locations around the ranch, and put the blocks in the middle of each pen. A month or so later, he went by to check on the blocks, and lo and behold, there wasn't a one left. Ya see, some cows had developed a taste for the blocks and had broken down the fences and eaten every one. This fella said it wasn't difficult to determine which cows did the damage, because within a few weeks, he had one cow with fourteen points and another with twelve. So he says those protein blocks really work—they'll grow the horns. Now if'n he can just build a cow-proof pen, he might have a few real trophy bucks running around on that place. And if he doesn't, he'll at least have some very unusual cows.

Anyway, talking about hunting and the outdoors is almost as much fun as being there. The other day, Tom Nowlin and I were working on a driveway project, and in less than two hours, we killed at least three elk and so many bucks no one would believe it. Some of these animals were dropped with offhand shots at a pretty fur piece. When one of us was talking, the other would be kinda looking at our feet, kicking a rock or two—you know, not really skeptical, but with a kinda Mona Lisa grin.

So since the bird season is here and the deer season is just around the corner, ya wanna be somewhat alert, vigilant, and cautious about some of the tales which might flow (particularly at a coffee shop) from an otherwise honest but enthusiastic Brush Country hunter. What I'm saying is that Brush Country hunters are almost as bad as most fisherpersons when it comes to getting their facts straight. Well, since he only saw that big ol' buck, fifteen points sounds better than ten,

Tommy Nowlin.

and since no one else was there, three hundred yards is a little more impressive than one hundred and seventy five, etc. But a prudent listener doesn't believe a Brush Country hunter anyway, and it's all in good fun. So you newcomers better keep this in mind. Hunters here are just like hunters any place you've ever been: enthusiastic.

Can't Shoot Worth a Flip?

With the beginning of deer season now just days away, some folks will be out sightin' in their muskets. A few will have difficulty in obtaining the accuracy they'd like. Occasionally they might think, *Well, the simple truth is, I can't shoot worth a flip.* Under the conditions in which they'd be shooting, that conclusion might be correct—because, ya see, there are many factors which affect accuracy, and not all of it has to do with the shooter's skill. So before ya run down to the Burnt Boot Bridge and try to end it all by jumping overboard, ponder these points.

Probably one of the more common causes of gross inaccuracy in rifle shooting is that the sighting system is deficient, and in most cases, this means the scope is misaligned or loose in its mounts or that the mount is loose. So ensure all sight attachment screws are snug.

Another reason why your grouping may not be very tight is that the stock and barrel on your ol' musket may not fit perfectly and only "come together" at the "high points." If ya try everything else I mention here and you are a good shot and ya still don't have the accuracy, this may be the problem. The only answer is to glass bed your stock, and you can do that with a kit.

Still another cause of inaccuracy is a cold rifle barrel, as it is when you fire your first shot at a target. When sightin' in and practicing, ya fire a number of shots one after another, and the barrel gets hot. With some expansion, the ol' bullets are apt to take off on a tangent.

If'n that isn't enough, consider this. You take two new rifles—same model, same manufacturer, same caliber—and fire the same kind of ammo. One will group well; the other will not. The reason is that each rifle is an individual. So the only way to find the best ammo is to hand load. Experiment with different powder, bullets, and primers and different weights of each. Then—and only then—you'll be able to find the best load for each musket.

HB sighting in his favorite muzzle loading shotgun.

Another reason why hand-loading is *the way* is because factory ammo is made to fit all of the many different types of actions and also to fit chambers with varying dimensions. The result is that factory ammo seldom fits any rifle perfectly—and some inaccuracy ensues.

That's not all. Let's say that the brand of ammo you use is produced by a firm that isn't much when it comes to quality control. Their bullets vary in weight by as much as a grain or so. That will have a significant affect on accuracy, as can an error of a grain or so in powder charge. Some companies guarantee their loads will not vary in powder or bullet weight by more than one tenth of a grain. These factors assume the gun is in good shape. If it is old—real old—and the barrel is all shot out, forget it. There's no way.

But now we must turn to the shooter. If your eye is good, you've got a steady hand, everything's coordinated, and you don't flinch, you should be capable of shooting accurately. But there are a few physiological factors to keep in mind. One has to do with breathing. When you get ready to shoot, you can easily quit breathing for a few counts, and that'll help ya hold a little more steady. But there's one thing you can't do, and that is shut down the ol' ticker. And if you don't think that makes a difference, crank that ol' scope up to nine power, sight in on something two hundred yards plus downrange, and watch what happens every time the ol' ticker ticks. I'll take that inaccuracy, though.

Just as soon the old ticker continues.

Elk Fever

I don't know about other hunters, but even though I've been at this business of hunting for over forty years, I still haven't shaken the ol' malady commonly referred to as "buck fever." To most experienced hunters, buck fever is the mark of a neophyte—a beginner, a greenhorn. But to me, buck fever is natural and real. It's brought on by a tremendous surge of anticipation and excitement. If it's just routine to stuff that ol' musket full of ammo, climb up in a blind, and bust the first horn-bearin' critter that comes along, well, forget it. It isn't worth the effort. It wouldn't be any fun, 'cause you need the proper amount of excitement.

Last month, I was out in the Rockies trying to "jump" an ol' bull elk. I wasn't too familiar with my hunting environs, and before daybreak on opening morn, I was kinda reclining on this hillside, freezin' and just mildly shaking. Some two hundred yards out in front was an area relatively clear of all brush; it was an ol' landslide area that began at the base of this steep slope and extended up to the rimrock another six hundred yards away. Anyway, as the sun rose and things came a little more into focus, I realized I was too far from the slide area. I rustled my bones and headed uphill. Nearer the slide, there was a rock about as large as an average living room, and I mounted that rock for a little better view of the countryside. The temperature that morning was about 24 degrees, and the rock was super-cooled. In about twenty minutes, the shakin' and shiverin' began and increased in intensity until the sun came up with some authority and kinda thawed things out. At about this time, I heard a noise up on the hillside at least three hundred yards out. It was unmistakable; it could only be one thing—a bull elk was comin' my way, and his rack was so huge and heavy, he was crashing into the top of every small oak within two feet on either side of him. He had to cross that clearing, except that there was a small strip of brush at the base of this side—but no sweat; he couldn't get through without my seeing him. I was ready with ol' reliable—a .338 Winchester magnum with hand-loaded 225-grain bullets at 2,900 feet per at the muzzle sighted in to be "on" at 250 yards.

But as that ol' bull "closed," the physiological phenomenon known as "buck fever" set in—or in this case, elk fever. At first I thought that landslide was starting all over again, but I soon realized that the clattering I heard was simply my teeth, and the rattlin'— well, that was only my knee bones hittin' that cold rock. So to make a long story shorter, that ol' bull is still out there somewhere. He marched right through all of that brush, somehow skipped through that narrow neck of woods, and made it safely to the other side. I don't have a big, impressive trophy to display. The elk still has it. But I'll never forget that experience, and I hope I never stop having buck fever, because if I do, it'll be a signal to hang it all up and go back to golf or some other pastime.

BRUSH COUNTRY BULL 1978

JANUARY 5, 1978

Slingshots

For most of my youth, a slingshot or two accompanied me just about everywhere I went. And those slingshots were homemade. We usually had a mesquite fork and rubber straps from an ol' automobile inner tube (all rubber and not synthetic) obtained free from any service station. The leather sling usually came from an old boot or shoe tongue. Cotton string was used for attaching the rubber, stock, and sling together, and that was supplied from Mom's kitchen drawer. Rocks always came from the road that ran in front of our home. The rocks had to be the right size and as round as possible, since a flat rock isn't ballistically effective. When hunting, my brother and I usually carried a spare slingshot around our necks, which supplied some extra string and a couple of rubber straps. We'd load each pocket with rocks and head up Chacon Creek looking for any kind of game, usually birds and snakes.

"Shucks, ya cain't kill a snake with one a' them things," scoffs the doubter. But I recall one Sunday afternoon when my brother, his friend, and I killed twenty-one snakes along the Chacon. Some of those were killed by the dogs that always followed us around, but we took our share, too.

One of my first big kills came out in the barnyard. I was about five, and Mom's ol' rooster and I had built up quite a hatred between us. Every time I walked through his territory, he'd come over and challenge me since we were about equal in size. Anyway, on this day, he came over to challenge me, and I had my shooter loaded. He kinda walked sideways up to me at a range of not more than twelve inches and stopped. At that point, I drew back all I could and let fly. It's hard to miss at that range, and the rock landed smack dab on the side of the rooster's head—end of challenge, end of conflict, end of rooster. When he quit flopping, I drug him over and hid him under the barn. Mom didn't ask, so I didn't see any point in confessing.

On occasion, when we wanted a change from the regular target, we would shoot our buddies with the shooters. We had regular wars with those things. Chinaberries were our ammo, and man, could that sting when ya got hit in the small of your shirtless back.

One of the dangers for beginning slingshot artists is that ya don't want to forget and release the wrong end of that thing. I had a great uncle on a family picnic who obtained a sling shot from of the youngsters and said, "Watch me hit that mule off down yonder in the field." He drew back all he could and let loose of the stock. The mule never knew he was in danger, but ol' Uncle Tobe wound up with not one but two knots on the head. Another thing—don't let your thumb stick up too high in the fork; some say that's a good aiming point. Ya can lose more thumbs that way.

Well, take it from me—sling-shooting was great fun! I always remember those hunts as a treasured highlight of my childhood.

Briscoe Talks about Oak Trees

Recently I learned that a druid (the modern-day variety) is one who worships oak trees. Today, America has some 5,000 members of the druid persuasion. The religious philosophy I follow differs somewhat from that used by the druids, but I can certainly understand their love of oaks, particularly if it's a live oak. Some may not know, but there are over sixty varieties of oak, most of which are not common to this area. Basically, oaks fall in two categories—they are either red or white oaks. Members of the red oak family may easily be distinguished because their leaves generally have pointed, bristle-tipped lobes. In this area, post oaks and chinquapin oaks are about all you'll find in the white oak family. In the red category, though, there are the shumard, blackjack, willow, laurel, and of course, our ol' live oak. As a member of the red oak family, the live oak doesn't have much of a bristle-tipped leaf, but it is in fact a member of the red oak family.

Anyway, in this area, the ol' live oaks are about the oldest living things. Down south of Devine a few miles nearer Moore-Holler, there's an ol' live oak standing alone out in a sandy field, and it must certainly be one of this area's largest trees. It's on the old Tom Rollins place, and it has a north to south spread of 116 feet. The circumference at its base is twenty-one feet, and it is approximately fifty feet high. That grand ol' oak takes up just about one fourth of an acre, and it absolutely dominates the surrounding area. When I look at it, I'm certainly happy no one ever saw fit to plow it up. I have no idea how old that tree is, but I'm guessing it's at least six hundred years old, maybe older. It just doesn't seem right that one person could determine that tree's longevity. Ya see, that tree was here long before anyone owned it. And barring disease or hardware problems,

The Tom Rollins Live Oak, struck and killed by lightning in the 1990s.

it'll probably be here long after you and I are gone. It—and many others like it—should be considered a national treasure, kinda like the redwoods, and maybe it ought to be against the law to destroy it. So don't get me wrong—currently no one intends to level that ol' oak, but someday, maybe far out in the future, there might be an owner who might determine it would be far better to quit plowing and planting around that old tree and just take it outta there. If so, that person should be tried and convicted of murder in the first degree.

FEBRUARY 23, 1978

Good Ol' Environmentalists

Some environmentalists would have American believe that we've just about consumed all our timber resources—that we've flat cut it all down to the bare nubbin. But let me tell you the straight skinny, having flown over just about every smidgen of Western America at low altitudes, and fairly recently—we ain't hurtin' when it comes to timber. You can't believe it, actually, unless you see it yourself—the Sierras in eastern California, Cascades in Oregon, Olympias in Washington, and many other areas, hour after hour at jet speeds—timber as far as the eye can see with practically no evidence of logging. If I had to take a guess, I'd say less than 1 percent has been harvested. Of course, some of that timber might be difficult to get a truck in to, but it's there.

The amazing thing is, did ya ever stop to kinda consider the number of telephone and power poles we use just here in the Brush Country? Thousands and thousands, and many of those telephone poles require one tree to the pole. It's wonderful that we have those resources in the tremendous amounts we do. But we still must be careful about their use. When an area is timbered, little seedlings must immediately be replanted. One reason we have so much timber at this late date may be because of some shrill environmentalists who agitated back a few years ago. We can be thankful that they were kinda shrill when trying to be heard. So really, I'm happy we have a few shrill environmentalists. Sometimes I'm even happy we have the Environmental Protection Agency. It's possible that one of these days, the EPA will divert their attention from conducting mileage tests on automobiles (which always result in their test automobiles getting anywhere from five to ten miles more than similar models sold to consumers) to something more important like launching a campaign to clean up America. We need an education program—and that's all it is—a matter of getting the word across to all Americans about littering, storing useless junk, and on and on. They could do a great service.

HB in the Sierras, 1975.

But my point is that environmentalists are not all bad. They provide a check and balance that's necessary. It's the "rebel without a cause" kind of environmentalist that can drive ya up a wall. When confronted with those types, they're easily recognizable; ya simply have to *press on!*

A Horse to Work and Play With

I once had a horse that chased rabbits—really. His name was Kayo, and Kayo arrived in this world when I was about five. At five years of age, I herded cows on this horse and rode his mother bareback before and after he was born. Ol' Kayo's genealogy wasn't much: Broomtail out of No-Show out of Glue-Factory out of Dog Food. But somehow, out of all that, Kayo was something. As horses went, he was a genius.

He'd hardly been weaned when Dad had some neighbors take and break him—and broke he was. When he returned, he was mine. We grew up together, almost constant companions. When I left for college, ol' Kayo was still out there on the farm.

Early in Kayo's life, he came when I called him—a few whistles, a few calls of "Here, Kayo," and he'd come running. I'd give him an ear of corn, and we'd ride. Pretty soon, he learned that an ear of corn wasn't worth whatever it was I wanted him to do, so he wouldn't come anymore. I'd have to go to him with the shuck rattling. Eventually, it would be too much, and he'd have to come over and have that ear of corn—and I'd catch him. We did that for a while, and finally he decided that even if I walked to him, the corn still wasn't worth it, and he wouldn't let me catch him. So Dad had three greyhounds, and I'd simply set those hounds on him. They wouldn't bite him but would bay him into the corner of a field, where he would inevitably give in. Then I'd bridle him.

Well, as Kayo got older, he really didn't care about working, and the thing he hated most was to move cattle from our home place down to another location in the blackjacks. But I had to go to the blackjacks almost every summer day to check for screwworms. Usually there'd be just Kayo and me, and if ya ever tried to drive twenty or thirty head of cattle through a crossroad when they didn't want to go and there's just you and the horse—that gets a mite tricky and takes some work and even more persistence. They'd cut one direction, and we'd be after them; but by the time we got back to the crossroads, the ones behind would be heading in still another direction. It was frustratin'. Eventually Kayo and I would win, and we'd head east with those cows. Now, if there was a young calf, and he wasn't moving along fast enough, Kayo'd put back his ears and nudge that calf along with his nose. Sometimes he'd nip a slow-moving cow. You'd almost have to club ol' Kayo to get him past the crossroad. But once we finished our chores at the blackjacks and ya closed the gate, hang on, because he'd light out for home, flat smoking!

Back in those days, every baby calf had screwworms in its navel if ya didn't administer a little Formula 62. So screwworm treatment was an everyday job that fell to me and Kayo. We had to catch the calves by roping them, and Kayo was a fantastic roping horse. If I'd been any good at roping and tying, we'd probably have done better in some of the local rodeos we entered. We did a lot of goat-roping, and I think that Kayo thought that was crazy—and it was. Those goats were flat unpredictable.

Another of Kayo's responsibilities was to get the car started in the winter. I'd saddle Kayo, tie a roping rope to the rear bumper, and Kayo'd pull the car out of the garage into the road. Then we'd hook him on to the front bumper and at a gallop he'd be going fast enough to get the car started at one horsepower—Kayo.

But back to rabbit-chasing. Kayo learned to do that because as we were going across the fields and pastures every morning and evening to bring in the dairy cows, the greyhounds would usually always be with us. So when a rabbit jumped, they'd be off with us right behind. If a rabbit jumped when the greyhounds weren't with us, look out! Ol' Kayo'd accelerate from zero to thirty in three seconds, and you'd be left on the ground flat on your back.

In those days, ol' Tharon Savage and I developed a little game we played with eight to ten other friends—touch football on horseback in a thirty-acre field. Talk about fun! Pretty soon, though, it wasn't much of a contest, because Ol' Kayo perfected a stiff arm—uh, stiff leg. When someone would come up behind him to tag, he'd come off the ground with both hind feet and let that ol' horse have it right in the whiskers.

Kayo and I had our tough times, too. Twice we were cutting cattle in a big lot behind our house when the manure-covered lot was wet. His feet left him, and we came down smack dab in the middle of a mud—uh, manure puddle. That didn't hurt much, but another time, the same thing happened, and this time we hit on hard ground, and his full weight landed on my leg. That smarted, and ol' Kayo did a little gasping before his breath came again.

Well, that Kayo was something; I loved that ol' horse and still do. It isn't often that one comes in contact with an animal with a personality like Kayo, and I'll never forget him.

Three Ol' Greyhounds

As I said not long ago, my father had three ol' greyhounds when I was a youngster, and those hounds were the source of much entertainment. One of my father's best friends was Mr. Alex "Dick" Bohl. The reason my father decided to get some hounds in the first place was because Mr. Dick had some, and Dad had seen them run. So anyway, Dad eventually obtained three hounds. One, Longboy, was a streamlined, sleek, jet-black animal that had the most beautiful conformation—a fantastic-looking animal. It was absolutely beautiful to see him run. Ya couldn't believe the speed he had. A number of times, I was in a position to see him run when I was at right angles to his direction of travel. With every stride, Longboy would seem to gain six feet or more on a rabbit; he'd flat close, and ya know when it comes to running, a jack ain't no slouch.

Then there was Gracey. She came aboard too when she was just about grown. And Gracey was appropriately named. Grace, agility, strength, speed—she had it all. Gracey was almost all white with just a few liver-colored spots. Sometimes ol' Longboy was a little lazy, but not Gracey. She always went along when I was on horseback, and many's the time she'd jump a jack and be after him. Ya just had to kinda stop and watch in awe as that animal set sail. She was beautiful.

Finally, there was ol' Jack. Jack was a greyhound, and that was about all ya could say about him. The fastest I ever saw ol' Jack run was when three coyotes chased him outta the brush north of our home place. Ol' Jack was flat smoking when he came by me, and he couldn't stop till he got home. Anyway, Jack was pretty good at runnin' wide to try and turn an ol' jackrabbit away from the brush. Ya see, a greyhound can't run in the brush; he runs by sight, for one thing, and the other thing is at that speed, he just couldn't handle it.

Well, anyway, sometimes on a Sunday afternoon, Dad and Mr. Dick would get together with their hounds and hunt some of the larger fields around these parts, and the fun would begin. I'll never forget that one of their favorite fields was down about where Lee Rackley lives southeast of Devine called the old Bailey place. The rabbits down there were exercised almost daily by the nearby hound population. Those rabbits were not only smart, but they also were almost as fast as greyhounds, and when ya jumped one of those critters, the race was on. As well as I could remember, most of those ol' rabbits in the Bailey place lived to a ripe old age, and I kinda think they looked forward to Sunday afternoons so they could test the skill and dexterity of all canine comers.

Now, if'n ya really wanted some thrill and excitement, take those hounds out in an oat patch some cool winter night. In those days, a patch could be home to fifty or more rabbits. There'd be so many, the hounds wouldn't know which one to chase. Sometimes each hound would have his own rabbit. When ya got a rabbit in the car lights, he'd go flat crazy, 'cause he'd see his shadow and would be apt to do almost anything. Sometimes the lights would blind him—blind the dogs, too—and that would be a zany chase. Those old hounds would come off the downhill side of a terrace, and they'd kind of lose their equilibrium and do some fancy acrobatics before coming back to earth. It was great fun, and I can hear my Dad now, hollerin' at those hounds. We didn't catch many rabbits, but we sure had fun. I kinda wish sometimes I could see ol' Longboy and Gracey run again and hear ol' Dad and Mr. Dick egging 'em on.

Cow Talk

Those of you who haven't been around cows much have missed a lot in life. When ya get down to it, cows have to be some of the most unusual creatures on earth. Personally, I really love those ol' bovines, but there are times if I had a club big enough … Anyway, if God didn't endow you with cow sense, forget it—you ain't never gonna have it. To know how to deal with cattle, one has to be around them a lot, and one has to have that cow sense I was talking about.

A cow has a strange anatomy. There's a muscle that runs directly from the tail to the brain. When she raises her tail, it disengages her brain. And worse, when she raises her tail, that's a signal to the others, and they are apt to raise theirs—and look out, those bossies are fixin' to launch in some direction, sans brains. But with cows, there's always exceptions, and if one of them ol' heel flies is bitin' at them, they'll sometimes raise their tails and usually dash under a mesquite tree. And if flies are the cause of their tail-raisin', the others won't usually follow suit. They'll know that it's just flies and ignore the signal.

Cows are gregarious; they have to be with other cows. They are also distrustful of one another. If they are all out grazing and one of them kinda raises her head and starts walking off, the others will follow. I suppose they think she has a secret grazin' place, and they want to check it out. Recently, a couple of my yearlings had crossed the fence over to a neighbor's field. I tried everything I could to drive them back, but no way. They were near the fence, and I had the rest of the herd just across on my side of the fence. Well, the solution to that problem was to get a handful of range cubes and lead the herd away from them. The two yearlings couldn't stand to be left alone and flat jumped over the fence. But with cows, there's an exception to every rule. If you're trying to get them all in a pen and ya get them all in but one and the last one decides you're trying to get her in that pen, she'll do everything she can to keep from being penned, even if it means separating from the others.

A cow is the only animal that can stand within five feet of an open sixteen-foot-wide gate and not see the opening but can look through the brush a half-mile away and spot a staple out of a fence post and within three minutes, crawl through the opening.

If there ever was a critter that could play the angles, it's a cow. If you're trying to drive one down a fence into a pen, ya gotta have the proper angle on her. If you're six inches too far to the left, she'll cut back to the right on you—and vice versa. And if ya crowd her too much, she'll turn and stand her ground. That means, "I ain't goin' in that pen." So when that happens, ya keep the proper angle and give a little ground—not much; just keep the pressure on her. Finally, she'll turn (maybe), and when she has her back to you, give more pressure, and she might eventually go into the pen … if you have the proper angle.

Mom B's heifers down by the Chacon.

There's something peaceful about a cow. There are times when my wife and I have to check on those bossies after dark. They'll be lying down, and when we drive up, they'll get up. Since they know my pickup, they'll come cruisin' over to see what gives. Really, they're looking for a handout of a range cube or two. So if ya don't have a range cube, they'll come right on up to you and at a distance of a foot or so, just stop—ears forward, looking right at you, chewin' that cud. They'll stand there as long as you have the strength. But better not take a stranger along. Cows can spot a stranger a mile off, and that makes them a little nervous.

Well, compared with some of the real cowpokes, I don't know much about cows, but I'm learning, and one of the things I find kinda hard to cope with is that it's hard to sell one of your friends. Really, it's easy to get attached to some of those critters when ya only have a few like I do, and I feel kinda bad when I have to load one of them sad-eyed, trustful bovines in the trailer and head to market. But then, there are some I can't wait to get in that trailer and get to market. Come to think of it, cows may really be a lot like people—stubborn, unpredictable, and loveable.

The Gooney Bird

Now here in the Brush County, one seldom (never) sees a Laysan albatross, and that's unfortunate, because when it comes to interesting and weird critters, the Laysan albatross ranks near the top. Seldom does anyone refer to them by their scientific name; it's always the gooney bird, and that's an appropriate name.

The gooney bird spends his winter on Midway Island northwest of Hawaii about 1,100 miles along with a few other islands in that vicinity. When living in Hawaii, I was working in flight safety, and the airport at Midway was one of my responsibilities. I soon became an expert on gooney birds, mainly because gooneys ain't afraid of anything, including airplanes. A ten-pound Gooney going 50 mph in one direction can do a real job on a ninety-ton airplane going 180 knots in the opposite direction. Jet engines don't particularly feed well on gooney bird feathers, flesh, and bones. So that's how I came to know those ol' gooneys first hand.

Now on the ground, gooneys are out of their element. Walking is a chore. They kinda move along bow-legged like and every now and then take a hitch or two. About every other step, their knee joints give way, and that gives them a crazy up-and-down motion. Their top speed is about 1 mile per hour when in a hurry. Now when they aren't in a hurry, they slow down considerably. Ya walk right up next to one, and he ain't about to hustle off. He'll just stand there looking sideways at ya. But if they're nesting or have young, it's best not get too close to that five-inch-long beak, 'cause he'll remove a portion of your anatomy.

A gooney's greatest moments of concern are when he takes off and lands—kinda like airplanes. Also like airplanes, an ol' gooney will taxi out to a more or less clear spot for the takeoff, and he also

The Quintessential Gooney

must get a running start to get his ground speed up before he effectively attains flying speed. If your legs are all messed up (as theirs are) and ya have a seven-foot wing span, taking off is difficult. Well, when everything's set, the ol' gooney will line up into the wind and then get to hobbling, hitching, stutter-stepping, and flapping those wings and finally get to liftoff speed. Then twenty feet out, he'll collide with a sand dune in an uncontrolled crash. He'll get himself back together, stand up, shake himself off, look around to see who was watching, and give it another try. Once airborne, he's a thing of beauty; a graceful, fantastic flyer. But when it comes to landing, look out again.

I think an ol' gooney learns to kinda get down close to the ground, get a grim look on his face, close his eyes, fold his wings, and wait for the crash. That's the best way. Others will come sailing along, though, look back, and seem to think, *Hey, I wanted to land back there* and try to make an instantaneous turn with a resulting cart-wheeling, end-over-end, crunching crash. But a gooney is tough, and Midway is mostly sand, so the only thing that's usually hurt is their pride.

The ol' gooney is smart, though. In the spring, when hatchin' and raisin' is done, at some signal, they all launch and head for the Aleutian Islands where they spend the summer. Somehow or other in the fall, despite a pea-sized brain, they'll head back across that 1,800 miles or more of ocean to where they were hatched. Those gooneys are something else—and so is nature.

Brush Country Tales—Tall and Short

Ya know, as time goes by and generations pass on, a fantastic amount of information (history) passes with those generations. It's never recorded. Sooner or later, though, the tales get a little warped—stretched—then eventually they're altogether forgotten. And that's a tragedy.

Anyway, every now and then, I intend to delve back into the past and review some of the incidents that happened in this area. At least they will have been recorded in writing. When I do that, there's no way I can vouch for accuracy. These events are—or will be—mostly passed on by word of mouth. So let's get on with it.

Well, way back there when I was a youngster, I heard about this incident many times from a number of sources—and maybe you've heard it, too. Ya know ol' Bigfoot Wallace loved this country, like many of us do, and he kinda hung his hat around these parts. One book about his life starts out when the writer meets Bigfoot at his cabin on the Chacon Creek. Now years ago, I heard from one source that this cabin was on the east side of Chacon Creek somewhere along about where the low water crossing is just east of the drive-in theater between Devine and Natalia. You can be certain that it wasn't down next to the creek, 'cause ya see, the ol' Chacon kinda gets out of its banks every now and then—way outta its banks. Maybe someone can pinpoint that cabin a little closer. Anyway, word has it that ol' Bigfoot was headin' east late one evening and came up the west slope of Morris Hill, 1.5 miles west of Devine. On top, looking east down to the Francisco, were Indians! About the time Bigfoot saw them, they saw Bigfoot.

So whatta ya do when there's twenty or thirty braves between you and your destination and you're alone? Well, ol' Bigfoot held on to his scalp fer a long time, so he musta had considerable grey matter between his ears. Story has it that he turned in his saddle, faced west, and began motioning like there were troops behind him. Then ol' Bigfoot charged the Indians, and they lit a shuck. Near the creek, Bigfoot made a sharp turn away from the Indians' trail and headed for home. True? I dunno. I've heard that story many times.

Now a different story—Mr. Jack Griffin (long deceased) was an early pioneer, and once when I was a small boy, he and my father were headin' north from the Black Creek Baptist Church. A mile or so north, there was an old swamp (now long since plowed up and made into a ground tank). But at that time, Mr. Jack was saying to my father, "Years ago, there was a massacre there in that swamp. Some families were attacked by Indians and took refuge there—drove their wagons right on out in the swamp for better protection. There were no survivors, and for years, the old wagons could be seen there."

Well, something that kinda ties in with that story is in that area; there is today clear evidence of an old trail—wagon or oxcart. Supposedly it went from Eagle Pass to San Antonio. In those days, trails led from one swamp to another. Remember, there are few permanent streams coming along northeast bound from the Hondo to the Medina, so those ol' swamps provided the necessary water for oxen and horses.

Well, it's only by word of mouth, except that I have seen evidence of the old trail. Trails connecting swamps make sense. The families could have been traveling the trail when attacked. That's all I know about those incidents. Maybe you might know more. If you do, let me know.

Pheasant Hunting on Cheju-Do Island

It's a fur piece from Brush Country to where there's good pheasant hunting, and it's *really* a fur piece from here to where the world's best pheasant hunting can be found. That place is Cheju-Do Island about twenty-six miles off the southern tip of South Korea. Sitting out in the Japan Sea, Cheju-Do is nothing more than an inactive volcano that rises to some 6,000 feet and covers an area of roughly thirty square miles.

During the Korean War, most of the prisoners taken by the United Nations forces were transported over to Cheju-Do to cool their heels in a POW camp. The US kinda maintained that POW camp, and we had an airfield down there. The local folks who lived on Cheju-Do were primitive—no vehicles; therefore, no paved roads, no electricity, and mostly they lived in rock huts. The island is there in the middle of the cold Japan Sea. It's frigid in the winter with one snowstorm moving in right after the other. But if it wasn't much of a place for human beings to live (and it wasn't), it was super-fantastic for pheasant—and deer. The local folk didn't hunt, so it was really unrestricted hunting—no season, no limits, no laws, but pheasants everywhere. On three separate occasions, I was fortunate enough to spend time on Cheju-Do hunting.

We'd land there on a grassy field in an ol' C-47 Gooneybird, pick up a couple of jeeps, load our gear and guns, and then head for about the two thousand-foot level. It was mostly open, grassy country with crumbling rock walls that had been constructed from rocks taken out of the fields. The pheasant were everywhere, and to a lesser extent, so were the deer. It wasn't uncommon to see four to five hundred pheasants on the rise. Our shotguns were unplugged, and if one could get on those ol' birds, ya could get maybe four birds when they were on the go. It wasn't bad shootin'! Once I spent three days there, hunted a couple of hours in the morning and something like that in the afternoon, and my take was around fifty birds.

Now if a person can't hit a pheasant, he can't hit anything. It's a big ol' bird, and it mostly flies in straight lines. But the main problem is that those big ol' birds can flat move out, and that's the reason some miss. They shoot where the bird was.

Chejo-Do Island Hunt.

There were many of these little ol' Roe deer. When we were pheasant hunting, we always carried two rounds of buckshot for ready use. Once I was slipping along and happened to see these two deer headin' my way. I quickly switched from bird to buckshot, and one came bounding up out of a draw through the heavy snow. I dropped that big ol' buck, and it field-dressed at fourteen pounds—a full-grown deer. Another time, I was deer hunting with my trusty 30-06 and dropped one of those big bulls from a distance of about ten yards. He dressed smaller—about twelve pounds. I should have had my .22.

Anyway, I'll always remember those hunting trips to Cheju-Do, and it was the only situation I ever knew of where military people left Japan and went to Korea for rest and recuperation. For me, there was no better R&R to be had anywhere than on Cheju-Do Island, climbing over the rock walls and wading through the knee-high dry grass and sometimes snow. But best of all was back in camp at night, sitting around the ol' camp stove with all the guys, talking over the day's hunt, and eating smothered pheasant and pan-fried venison backstrap—just kinda living. That Cheju-Do was a great place.

Indians Kill Joe Wilton in Devine

One mile east of Devine—before there was a Devine—Dan Patterson had a ranch in the 1870s. And early on the morning of April 22, 1877, young Joe Wilton, eighteen, caught up his horse, saddled him, and lit a shuck from the Patterson ranch westbound for Hondo Creek. He was headed for the Segenus Store, which was at the Hondo Creek crossing of the Eagle Pass-San Antonio Trail. Joe Wilton didn't make it.

Late that afternoon, Joe's widowed mother became concerned. Joe should have long since returned. So she contacted some neighbors, one of whom was Bee Tilley. Some of the Tilleys lived close by under an oak grove now about 260 yards southeast of the Natalia/Bigfoot Road overpass of I-35. Then someone also contacted Rufe Ketchum, who lived in the Blackjacks about three miles east of current-day Devine. Approaching sundown, Bee and Rufe headed for a camp meeting being conducted by Rev. Hukill (later to become the first pastor of First Baptist Church Devine) since they thought Joe may have stopped by for the meeting. Rev. Hukill indicated that he had not seen the boy, but some fellas with "tin pans on their arms" had carried off all of his horses that day—tin pans on their arms meaning shields, which meant *Indians*. At sunset, Bee and Rufe set out for the store, concerned about Indians—and Joe Wilton.

At the store, long since dark, no one had seen Joe Wilton. Neither had anyone seen him at Lon Moore's ranch down the Hondo from the Segenus store. Bee and Rufe turned back toward Patterson's ranch and arrived at sunup. They picked up more help—the Tilleys, Moores, Frank Jackson, and Rufe—mounted, and started west. At Hondo Creek, they struck the Indians' trail and followed it to the Black Creek headwaters, now about six miles due south of Dunlay.

The Indians were headin' out of the country and were hours—almost a day—ahead.

Rufe, Bee, and the boys turned back. Some went back to the store, and others drifted down Black Creek. About four miles down the creek, they picked up the Indian trail again. This time, the Indians were chasing a lone horseman up the hill eastbound out of Black Creek valley, now at the crest of that range of low hills running north and south. That's just three miles west of Devine. Coming downhill, the Indians closed on the already-wounded Joe Wilton and finished the job. Under an oak, the tracking party later found Joe Wilton's arrow, lance, and bullet-ridden body—supposedly the last settler killed by the Indians in this area. The spot where Joe fell is marked even today by a pile of rocks. It's just out State Highway 173 a piece.

Joe Wilton's body was brought home in a wagon driven by Bee Tilley. Today you can see his gravesite in the southeast section of the Devine Evergreen Cemetery. His tombstone, flush-mounted with the ground, is inscribed with the words "KILLED BY INDIANS."

Recently, Arnold Griffin, Burney Driscoll, and I searched for an hour or so and failed to locate the pile of rocks that mark the spot where Joe Wilton fell. Arnold was told many of the details by his father, who said that a few days after Joe Wilton was killed, an Indian was killed near Cotulla with Joe's jacket on. Arnold remembers Joe Wilton's brother, who later lived in San Antonio. Many of those mentioned here have descendants in this area: the Tilleys, Rev. Hukill, Nettie Petri, and Kathryn Bywaters.

One of these days, we need to erect a historical marker out near where Joe Wilton fell right alongside Highway 173.

The Legend of G. W. Gardner

Back in the good ol' days (in the early thirties), my father, his brother, and Mr. Jim Burns used to pass through downtown Bigfoot en route to the Burns Ranch for dove hunting. I remember so many times hearing my father say, as we passed near the southern outskirts of Bigfoot, "Ya see that old gentleman sitting on the porch there?"

I'd say, "uh-huh."

He'd say, "That's Mr. J. W. Gardner—he was an Indian-fighter. Was wounded by the Indians."

Mr. Gardner was the father of "Pete" Gardner and grandfather of Flo Gardner, who works in the Devine city office. He was born in Louisiana in 1851, and his father settled in Atascosa County in 1855. In 1869, they settled in Bigfoot. Then in 1871, Gardner and two brothers were hired out to drive cattle down to the Nueces River near Cotulla. About a week after arriving on the Nueces, young Gardner went out on foot early one morning, unarmed, to look for some horses that were to be used in working cattle. About a half mile from the ranch house, he met a rather weird-looking character on horseback. Gardner thought it might be an Indian and turned to run. The fella shouted in Spanish for him to stop. Gardner looked back over his shoulder at the character who had on a big hat, a bow in one hand, and an arrow in the other. At this point, there was no doubt as to the horseman's intentions, and Gardner increased his withdrawal speed toward the house. But the Indian was mounted, and as he drew near, he fit the arrow to the bow and let it fly. The arrow shot clean through Gardner's left arm and into his side. Even worse, twelve more Indians, all on horseback, appeared and began to form a circle around Gardner, who promptly took cover in a clump of persimmon bushes.

One Indian rode up close and asked for Gardner's hat, motioning for him to run toward the ranch house. Looking in that direction, Gardner saw what appeared to be the chief and decided that wouldn't be such a good idea. But he did spot an opening and made his break while trying to yell loud enough to attract the attention of the people at the house. While trying to make his break on foot, another arrow struck. This one was under the right shoulder blade, and then the Indian who shot the arrow ran his horse over Gardner.

Somehow getting back to his feet again, Gardner once more called for help, and this time, people at the ranch house heard and responded. At this point, the Indians no longer tried to conceal their presence by shooting arrows and opened up with pistols. One pistol ball struck Gardner in the neck and came out under his jaw. Finally, the ranch hands arrived and drove the Indians off. Gardner had been wounded three times and had a total of seventeen holes made by bullets and arrows in his clothing. It was six weeks before young Gardner was sufficiently recovered to travel back to Bigfoot.

Well, that was one experience in the life of J. W. Gardner and serves to indicate what a dear price our ancestors paid in taming this country. I certainly admire and respect the people who settled this country, and I love our heritage. I hope that in the future, those who live in this country can show a little more of the pioneer spirit—particularly when conducting the affairs of this nation.

Dogs and Dawgs

I dunno if you've thought about this or not, but there's a great difference between a dog and a dawg. For some ten years now, my family has included a dog. We also have a dawg, but he's only been with us for a coupla months. Anyway, our dog is named Jacques, pronounced precisely like the term now used when referring to an athlete. Jacques is a miniature French poodle, and folks have asked, "What are you doing with a poodle? You don't look like the type. A cur dog would be more like it." Well, if you live up north in the cold country and want a small dog that lives in the house, doesn't shed hair, doesn't smell, and is intelligent, ya get a miniature poodle.

In his younger days, ol' Jacques could learn a trick in about fifteen minutes, and he still can perform them all, even though there may be times that he doesn't do them for four or five months. He's smart and a real gentleman. You could set food on the floor, and he wouldn't bother it. Also he disengages his barker when we go to bed. When a member of the family is gone for over two days and returns, he gives them his best welcoming performance—goes into a barking and running fit and keeps it up for three or four minutes. Even if you're gone for a year or so, he'll remember and go into his act; it's rewarding. He has even recognized some of our long-time close friends and does his act. Jacques has been separated from his family for only two or three nights in his life. Where we go, he goes.

Now not long ago, another canine character showed up here. He's a full-blood black and tan rat terrier. When he came here, he'd obviously been terribly abused and was wild as a March hare. Because of this extraction, we named him Quixote pronounced kee-OH-tay. When he came here, Quixote was so thin that he could step on a postage scale and the needle wouldn't move. He took up residence in a culvert which passes under the Yancey highway, and if he happened to be in the yard when someone came out of the house, he'd split and literally fly. About five hundred yards out, he'd stop and look back, but then by degrees, he became more gentle. Soon he'd only run four hundred yards, then 250, and so on until he'd stop in a hundred yards or so.

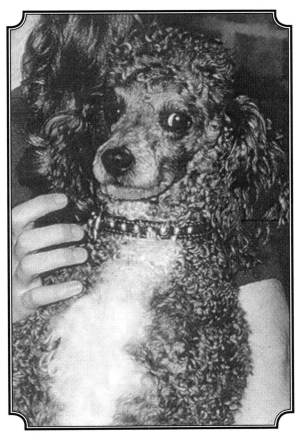

Jacques, 1967.

Well, we already had a dog and didn't care for another. So Quixote was determined to survive on his own. But when you're ten inches tall, raiding garbage cans is difficult when the top of the can is two feet higher than you are. But Quixote did it. Somehow he'd knock the top off and then flat jump up in the can. Sometimes he'd be out of sight, but about every ten seconds or so, that head would pop out. He'd take a look around, drop back in, and get on with the raiding. Quixote actually lost weight, and I couldn't stand it. When we started feeding him, he became a little more gentle and quit raiding garbage cans. He gained weight, but he still didn't want to be touched. He kept his distance.

He's now gained some self-respect, and every time anyone goes out in the yard, he's there. He'll stay with you as long as you're there. If he can discern which way you're gonna walk, he'll get out in front, kinda prancing and proud. That's really a strange sight, because when he was undergoing the abuse that made him like this, someone apparently slammed a door on his tail, and when he's marching northward, his ol' tail comes straight up for about two inches then makes a 90 degree turn and points due west. Ya kinda want to look over in that direction to see what he's pointing at.

Anyway, Quixote is a dawg. He lives outside, digs holes up next to the house so he can stay cool on hot days, tears up the paper in the mornings, and skips off with absolutely everything left outside for even just a minute—shoes, ropes, or even a screwdriver. He doesn't bark too much in the daytime, but at night, any and everything that moves is duly noted by ol' Quixote—but then, that's what a dawg is supposed to do.

The Good Ol' Days

Merle Haggard, my favorite country and western singer, has a song, "I Think We're Living in the Good Ol' Days." The message he conveys, in my judgment, is pretty close to being right, because I can well remember what many old-timers consider to be the "good ol' days," and just for the benefit of the younger folks, here's what the good ol' days were like for my mother.

My mother was Flora Hansel, later Flora Hansel Briscoe. Her friends called her Flossie. After graduating from the College of Industrial Arts in Denton (now Texas Women's University), Mom came to Devine as Devine High's first home economics teacher. That was in about 1914 or so. Later she was Harris County's first Home Demonstration agent in Houston. Also, she may have been Devine High's first and only female coach for the boys' varsity basketball team. Mom came here to teach, found her feller, and was about to get married when World War I interrupted her plans. So the minute Dad returned from France, they married in San Antonio. After a few moves, they finally settled in on a farm east of Devine in 1926. Not long after they settled, the Depression came, and here's how it was.

In the good ol' days, there was no electricity for those living outside the city. No big deal, huh? Not much until ya stop to consider no lights, no washer or dryer, no air conditioning or central heat, no electric iron or hair dryer, no mixer, no refrigerator or deep freeze, no vacuum cleaner, no water heater, and no microwave or electric stove. Now that puts things in a little different perspective. Well, Mom had a wood stove, and whenever it came mealtime, she had to fire up that ol' stove. Meal time came often, because when ya work from daylight to dark, ya eat three squares. In the wintertime, that wood stove was wonderful—warm and cozy. Come summer, though, it wasn't so wonderful. It was terrible. In July—canning and preserving time—the temperature outside would be 100 and 95 percent humidity. Inside, the kitchen temperature would be 135 with 100 percent humidity. There stood Mom, right by that hot cast iron stove with the peach preserves steaming, stirring, straining, dipping, tasting, and soaking, dripping wet.

Mondays were set aside for washing. All Mom did was drag up a few mesquite logs around the wash pot, build a fire, and heat the water. No Boy Scout could build a fire as quickly and effectively as Mom. She had the experience. When the water boiled, she took a bucket and filled her trusty ol' washing machine. I say trusty because mechanically, it never broke down. Ya see, it was made of cypress wood and was hand-operated. Ya pushed and pulled that hand crank to move the agitator. That provided little entertainment, and there just wasn't one load to push and pull on. It was a week's wash—load after load—that took most of the day. The ironing then came on Tuesday. In the wintertime again, it was cozy around that old wood stove. But in summertime, it wasn't much fun standing next to that stove, and ya have to have the stove going to heat the flat irons.

An everyday chore in addition to the cooking and house-cleaning was in the milk shed. It was twice daily, since cows—the dairy types—have never been bred to recognize weekends or holidays. Three hundred and sixty-five days a year, Mom was in that milk shed, cleaning the cans and bottles, washing the milk buckets, straining all of the milk, and pouring the milk in the containers. Sometimes she also operated a hand-cranked cream separator. And of course, Mom operated the butter churn—an ol' crock with an up-and-down dasher.

Sewing was a big thing in our household, and Mom did it all on a sewing machine—the pedal type operated by foot power. In the wintertime, Mom's north Texas female relatives would sometimes come down for a few weeks, and they'd sit in my parents' bedroom, let down the quilt on a ceiling frame, and sew on it in the middle of the day and talk.

George T. and Flora Briscoe, 1953.

Mom also had a few additional duties. She usually cleaned all the game and fish and also served as nurse and family doctor. In those days, ya didn't run to the doctor every time some kid got the sniffles. Ya put him to bed with a flannel rag on his chest and a good dose of Black Draught, and that cured anything. Mainly it cured someone from claiming to be sick when that someone wasn't. Ya gotta be near dead before you'll take your second dose of Black Draught. Anyway, Mom was a good nurse—kind and sympathetic. It was a pleasure to be sick (except for the Black Draught). Her other duties included taking care of some laying hens, helping butcher when we killed hogs or a calf, and taking care of the yard.

Well, somehow or other, Mom found time to teach a Sunday

school class, remain active in the PTA, and serve as our room mother. But there were some things Mom wouldn't do. She would not ride horseback, and she refused to milk a cow.

That's about the way it was for Mom in the "good ol' days." She never said much about being liberated. In fact, it was kinda the other way around. Later in life, when she came to visit my family, she'd be chomping at the bit to get back home after three or four days so she could tend to her chores.

Mom's contemporaries know about the good ol' days and the work and hardship, but in so many ways, those were really the good ol' days. There was more honesty. Ethics meant something. You cared for your neighbor, and since there was no TV or telephone, ya kinda had time to accomplish something. Today, America could use a revival of good aspects of the good ol' days, which should include a four-letter word—*work*.

Prognosticating Rain

Well, the dove huntin' ain't much, so I will address a subject which is very often discussed in this part of the world: *rain*. Really—the forecasting thereof or prognosticating. "Say, how in the world can a feller tell when it's gonna rain, anyway?" "Simple, just watch the 10:00 news." Trouble is, them fellers don't like to go out on a limb much, and they'll kinda say, "Well, the chance of rain is 30 percent through tomorrow evening." Now that's fairly broad, and that forecaster has pretty well covered his tracks.

Another way of looking at that is there's a 70 percent chance it ain't gonna rain. Then too, if'n it rains one tenth of an inch somewhere near Luckenbach, then he kinda hit his forecast, didn't he? So those fellas are pretty well covered—ya can't pin them down. There's hardly a way for them to miss a forecast. Hardly—but they do.

But if you really want to know if it's gonna rain or not, forget the 10:00 news, and watch nature instead. It's more interesting and maybe even more accurate. Anyway, ya see a bunch of snails heading for higher ground. What gives? Well, it's gonna rain, of course. There's something in that snail's tiny nervous system that says, "Hey, dummy, better start climbing or you'll drown." Of course, a never-fail (sometimes) method of forecasting rain is by watching the moon—particularly a new moon. It never rains in a full moon (well, usually never). So no use watching a full moon, 'cause it won't tell ya anything. It's a new moon that knows. Sometimes a new moon will be cupped so's it'll hold water. That's a bad sign—means dry, because no water can pour out. But if'n the new moon is tilted so's water can pour out, start hunting the high ground with the snails, cause it's gonna come a frog-strangler. That's true in Calama, Chile (where there has never been rain recorded), and it's also true at Mt.

Waialeale in Hawaii, where the average annual rainfall is 486 inches. I reckon it's true, 'cause the same moon shines in both places. It's just that at Mt. Waialeale, one is seldom able to see the moon, because it's obscured by the rain and clouds—and when it rains 486 inches a year, who cares, anyway?

Well, another method is by listening for the "rain crow." Now the rain crow is nothing more than a yellow-billed cuckoo—a character you're far more apt to hear than see. There's no way I can tell you in writing how a rain crow sounds. If'n ya don't know, you'll just have to go ahead and get wet with the rest of the dummies. Anyway, when ya hear a rain crow—which doesn't crow, but kinda cackles (or chuckles)—it's gonna rain, shore enough.

But just remember who's a cuckoo when ya hear the rain crow and want to put your money where your mouth is.

Now here's a bona fide, foolproof method (usually) of forecasting rain. Simply watch the cenizo bushes. When they flower in full bloom, you'd better break out the life jackets and boats, 'cause ya may be needing them. There's something somewhere in that ol' gray plant that can sense when it's gonna rain, and it lets you know in a beautiful sort of way. I only wish peaches and pecans were also endowed with that characteristic and would bear peaches and nuts when it was gonna rain.

Well, since it's dove season, you're driving along and see this ol' dove sittin' up there on this highline. She's got her body all outta shape—contorted, one wing sticking out—and she's reaching back to her tail for something. What's going on? Well, any outdoors nut can tell ya that it's gonna rain. This small voice has come to that ol' dove and said, "Uh, if you don't get them feathers oiled up, you ain't gonna be able to fly when it rains, and it's gonna rain real soon." And that's why that dove was oiling her feathers.

Well, those are just some of nature's indicators—and there are more: tree frogs croaking, a hog carrying a stick in his mouth (sure thing), and cows running, jumping, and playing (a wet norther). So there's any number of indicators; ya just have to be alert and look for them. Now if the time ever comes when ya see the snails heading for the high ground, the moon is wet, the rain crow is clucking, cenizo bushes are blooming, birds are oiling their feathers, tree frogs are croaking, and hogs are carrying sticks in their mouths—whew! You'd better board up the windows, anchor the house, and head for the high hills, 'cause the heavens is gonna open up—really.

Them Infernal Horseless Carriages

Over the years, there have been a number of inventions which have radically changed the way of life for most Americans, and that certainly includes folks here in Brush Country. Television has brought on change (unfortunately, much of it not necessarily good, in my opinion). Also, airplanes, computers, fast food, and many other "essential elements" have contributed to what is now a hurried and hectic lifestyle. But the one innovation that has brought on the most dramatic change has to be the automobile. When I was a youngster, I heard many a tale about some of the early experiences folks had with automobiles.

The first autos showed up here in the very early 1900's. Not long after their arrival, a prominent farmer south of Devine bought a new Franklin. The Franklin had a chain drive, and of course, no one in the family was experienced at driving that or any other machine. Shortly after the purchase, the family went downtown on a Saturday afternoon to shop and visit, which was a tradition in those days. The only one of the family who could drive the contraption was the teenage son. He and his friends decided to go into Castroville, which left dear ol' Dad to drive the rest of the family home. Here was the plan: the boy would get the car started for Dad, then all Dad had to do was steer the car toward home after the teenager jumped out. This sounded like a fine plan to all concerned and things went according to plan until Dad had to make a turn into the dirt drive up to the family farm. He mostly made the turn but clipped a fence, which got caught in the chain drive. Dragging the fence behind him, he neared the house but didn't know how to stop. So he made an abrupt turn and headed toward an open field, still dragging the fence and snapping off fence posts one after the other.

Now in a near panic, he just began circling. The wire fencing simply clogged the chain drive, and the infernal machine ground to a halt. Ol' Dad wouldn't allow anyone to drive that machine again. It was too dangerous, wouldn't stop when ya hollered "Whoa!" and had too many other disadvantages. The ol' Franklin sat out in that field for years.

Well, cars still weren't too sophisticated in my early days, and I can remember some kinda shaky experiences. In my earliest memory, we had a Model T Ford pickup truck. It was the favorite and only color that they made at the time—black. There was no top, and ya kinda climbed aboard, because the driver sat high off the ground. So late one evening, Mom was at the controls, and the two of us were just completing a turn to the north off

HB and his mother, known as Mom B, 1969.

College onto Old Highway 81. Suddenly the steering wheel came off in Mom's hands! Mom kinda went into shock while making some wild gyrations up in the air with the steering wheel. So we softly crashed into the broomcorn shed alongside the railroad tracks.

At that point, I was a little suspicious of Mom's driving ability. I now realize it was unfounded, because a short time later, the same thing happened. This time we ran into a ditch. The real clincher came on Saturday evening. All the chores were done, and we were headed into town. It was near dark, and we were just about to cross the railroad tracks when we heard a train coming. Mom's first thought was "we can make it." Her second thought was "no, we can't make it" … and so on, until the train was upon us and she made a Herculean effort to turn the car north along with the train in between the tracks and the broomcorn shed. Wow! Ever see and hear an ol' steam engine freight train going 60 mph from three feet? That did it. From that point on, I refused to ride with Mom.

Well, those were interesting days. Mom really wasn't that bad a driver. The most serious accident she ever had was hitting the broomcorn shed, and that wasn't her fault. The best part about those days was listening to the stories people had to tell. It was better'n TV.

Devine—A Historical Community

Recently I've spent considerable time in review of A. J. Sowell's two volumes of *Early Settlers and Indian Fighters of Southwest Texas*. From this source, it's apparent that this part of the Brush Country may have had more conflict between settler and Indian than almost any other section of the state. As I indicated earlier, A. J. Sowell was an Indian-fighter turned writer and spent much time in the 1890's visiting with many of the old pioneers and recording first hand their description of the many Indian encounters. The only community rating specific comments from Mr. Sowell was none other than Devine, and here's what he said.

"Thirty-three miles southwest from San Antonio is the flourishing little city of Devine in Medina County. It was named for Judge Devine of San Antonio long before the wail of a locomotive was heard in this country. The pioneers had erected their cabins here and commenced that long, desperate struggle with the savages for mastery in which civilization, in the end, was destined to triumph.

"Now, instead of the yell of the Comanche, Lipan, or Kickapoo is heard the scream of the steam engine, and the trail of the Redman is covered along the graded track by the right of way. In a radius of twelve miles of this place covered by portions of Frio and Medina counties, many bloody encounters took place. Nearly every hill, valley, branch, creek, or mott of timber is historic. Many graves are shown here and there and the traveler is told, 'they were killed by Indians.' Many of these old settlers still survive who escaped the arrow, bullet, lance, or tomahawk, and among these at the time of which I write (1897) were Tom Galbreath, Lon Moore, Sam McCombs, Gip Tilley, Bee Tilley, J. W. Winters, Big Foot Wallace, Thomas A. James, John Craig, Tobias Long, James Long, West Davidson, Holly Laxon,

George Crawford, James Crawford, Mrs. Amanda Long, Aunty Peggy Halsel, Mrs. Minerva Laxon, Rev. Newton, Reese Moore, W. M. Bramlett, Mrs. Anna Burch, Mrs. Sarah Smith, George McCombs, and many others."

Many of the Indian conflicts Mr. Sowell described took place at Hondo Creek. At least three battles occurred a coupla miles south of Devine where the Francisco and Chacon come together to form the San Miguel. In addition to those battlegrounds, there are the old trails or roads. The San Antonio to Eagle Pass road crosses Highway 173 within a stone's throw of the northbound turnoff to the sanitary fill some three to four miles west of Devine. I believe that the railroad runs alongside the old San Antonio to Laredo trail—the one used by Santa Anna and his troops on their way to the Alamo in February 1836.

Probably the main reason why so many scrapes took place in this immediate area was that in the early 1850's, settlers began to establish themselves along the Hondo. Then, as dug wells became fashionable, settlers began to dot the landscape at locations isolated from other settlers. This made them vulnerable to attack from Indians out of the northwest on raids mostly to increase their horse holdings.

So since the settlers were so isolated and vulnerable, more attacks occurred. But those folks hung tough, and they are the ancestors of many of today's Devine residents.

Broom Corn Pullin'

When I was growin' up on the farm, there were some chores of which I wasn't too fond—for example, milking those ol' cows when it was cold and raining and the cow lots were knee-deep in mud. That wasn't much fun. Neither was shocking hay very entertaining. Take an ol' patch of redtop cane two feet over your head, cut it with the horse-drawn mower, rake it with a horse-drawn rake into the windrows, and then ya kinda separate the windrows with pitchforks into shocks. But after being raked, that cane had become all entangled and ya could almost be hernia-bound before completing the first shock. After the hay stayed in shocks for a while, you'd then put it in the big haystacks. Two ways of getting the shocks into the haystack area were: first ya could use a bullrake, which was nothing more than 4x4s sharpened at the front end and fastened together with a 2x4 sticking out of the back. With a team pulling it as ya approach a shock, ya kinda raised up on the 2x4, and it would slide in under the shock, and you'd just haul it on to the haystacks. As you came near and lift the 2x4 again, the sharpened ends would dig in, and the rake would go tail end over teakettle and dump the shock; then you'd go back and get another.

That wasn't too bad. But the other way was to have a wagon configured with a hayrake. One man was on the wagon—the stacker—and probably two were on the ground. The loaders would approach a shock and load it on by pitchfork. But on the north side of our home place—back against the mesquite and heavy brush—rattlesnakes lived in the shocks, because field mice also lived there, and every rattler loves mice. At times, we'd have to abandon shocks in that area. Every shock would have one and sometimes two rattlers. When ya pick up a forkful of hay and throw it up to the stacker and halfway up the old rattler gets all irritated and starts rattlin', guess what the stacker does. No matter how high the stack, he leaps for his life over the far side. Then ya have to unhitch the horses and keep punching around on the hay with the forks till ya locate the rattler and kinda unload him and keep going. That was exciting, but after a while, one wanted to do something else.

The worst chores of all had to do with the broomcorn business—at least the way we did it in those days. Broomcorn grew best on heavy black land, and we had it in spades. In a good year, that ol' corn would be two feet over your head when ready to harvest. It always was ready to harvest on July 4. And in July, it can begin to get warm in the Brush Country—over 100 degrees with 99 percent humidity. Here you are, in the middle of the broomcorn field, where the chaff from broomcorn seed is ten times worse than the worst itching powder. There was no way you could tighten your shirtsleeves and collar sufficiently to keep out the chaff. The itch was so bad that at times, a rash would break out on my leather boots. After about two hours, you couldn't stand it any longer, and you'd break in a run for the Chacon, peel, and jump straight out into the middle of that ol' creek. What a relief—the water was cool and the itch was soothed right there in the middle of the mud, turtles, snakes, and frogs. It was heaven.

Anyway, the way you went at this business of pullin' broomcorn was that you'd reach up there, grab that offshoot leaf in your left hand with the broomcorn head in your right, and pull in opposite directions. The head would peel down and snap off at the first joint, and you'd go on to the next stalk and the next until ya had a handful—then you'd step on a coupla stalks, bend them over in the row, and lay the heads on those stalks. Then a fella would come along behind you and take the heads up in small bundles of about four or five inches in diameter. If'n you was well-heeled, you'd use string binder twine or such to tie it with, but if you were like us, you'd use string made from the leaves of dagger cactus. I can still smell the scent of that ol' cactus string.

Well, when the corn was tied in bundles, along came some fellers with a wagon, and they loaded the broomcorn onto the wagon. After ya got the mules or horse headed down the row where there was no driver, you simply hollered at the team to get them going or stop. When loaded, you'd head for the barn where the broomcorn bundles were placed on drying racks to cure. That was real fun up there in the loft of that barn topped with sheet iron. Throwing those bundles up at you, chaff everywhere, no wind—horrible. You had to put the corn on racks, because if you didn't, it was so green and moist that it would combust spontaneously, and you'd burn the place down. But sometimes it wouldn't dry so quickly, and you'd take it all out of the barn and put it on the fences around the place so the wind and sun would dry it faster. You had to just get it all out, and when a thunderstorm came, you worked like fury to get it all back in the barn before it got rained on and ruined. It was great sport.

When it was finally cured, you'd contact the threshing crew, and they'd come in. They'd bring their ol' truck, pulling this weird-looking contraption behind. They'd set up out in the lot, jack up a rear wheel of the truck, put a belt on the wheel, and then put the other end of the belt on a pulley attached to the thresher, which was nothing more than a framework with a wooden elongated cylinder with metal spikes sticking out. When the cylinder turned at the right speed, the threshers held the broomcorn bundles with the seed end against the spikes, peeling off the seed. Eventually, after the truck radiator overheated ten or twelve times, you'd be through threshing, and finally the baling would be completed, and the buyer would come out. "Oh, George, that corn ain't too good; stem's a little short (or too long). Looks like it's been rained on; there's some red splotches on it—we can't pay you too much for that kinda corn."

Even after that bad news, the job wasn't done. The seed made pretty good feed, so you had to get a shovel or two, a wagon, and a team and haul it into storage—more sweat, more chaff, more itch. If'n it came down to one reason why I chose to fly airplanes for a living, I'd probably have to say, "It's got something to do with that infernal broomcorn."

Texas and Brush Country is Better

If'n Brush Country weren't such a great place to live, I reckon I'd have settled up yonder in the northwest in Washington, the Evergreen State. For those of you who haven't been there, the Evergreen State ain't by any stretch of the imagination all covered by evergreen. As a matter of fact, all of central and most of southeastern Washington could best be described as a desert. They only get about seven or eight inches of precipitation per year, and half of that is in the form of snow. But no matter—Washington is a great place. That desert is full of pheasant, chucker, doves, quail, partridges, ducks, geese, and fish. As you probably guessed, the fish are in lakes, and there are plenty of lakes in that desert. Even a sorry fisherman like myself was able to limit out on more than one occasion. Those rainbow trout will spoil ya for any other kind of fishing. It's super.

Anyway, southeast and central Washington is greatly disadvantaged by being east of the Cascade Mountains. The midwinter temperatures plummet out of sight. For me, 25 degrees below zero is a mite too chilly, particularly when it stays down there for a coupla weeks. And come October, it can get real chilly—I mean cold—up in them mountains on a deer hunt. I've suffered through deer hunts in 15 degrees at the six thousand-foot level. Even in May out there in the flatlands, some of the larger lakes are still frozen over, and that ain't no good.

The only outdoor sport worth anything in the northwest in midwinter is ice fishing. However, only a registered idiot would do that. The temperature is a predictable ten, fifteen, or twenty below (or worse if you consider the wind chill). If you're not a registered idiot, here's the drill on ice fishing: ya drive right on out there over the ice. It's two feet thick or more, but no sweat; it'll hold your car. There's plenty of cars already out there. Pull up to a likely-looking spot, take out your ol' crowbar, and start chopping and poking until you break into clear water. The water fills the hole up, and now you're ready—only thing is, you're dad-burn freezin'. So get back in the car, start the engine and heater, and thaw yourself and the engine out. Okay, ready. Step out there with rod and reel in hand and drop that line in the hole. *Clunk!* The line didn't go anywhere, 'cause the hole froze up again. Coupla kicks, and it's open again. Now drop that ol' line in there with a salmon egg on the hook, and *wham*—an ol' rainbow has got it. Pull him outta there; then take him off the hook and toss him out on the ice. In ten minutes, he's quickly frozen stiff. After about fourteen "quick freezes," ya load up those frozen fish and head to the house. If it weren't for the cold, ice fishin' would be great.

But hunting is something else. I can still remember my favorite deer hunting place. It's up Stormy Mountain on the east slope of the Cascades just south of Lake Chelan. Ya drive along the lake's south shore until you come to Twenty-Five Mile Creek. Just past the creek, the pavement ends. Take a hard left on this dusty road which leads right up the creek. But as ya make that left-hand turn, there's a red delicious apple tree standing there. Now apple trees produce best when elevated in a cool climate and watered by cold, clear mountain water. Whatever else it takes to turn out a perfect apple, that ol' tree had it. The fruit would be in its prime when we made the turn up that dusty road the second weekend in October. Ya *have* to stop and sample some of the fruit from that tree every time. You could hear the *crack* off the canyon walls when you bit into one. The juice would run down your arm and drop off your elbows. We'd take enough apples to last the hunt and head on up the creek about five more miles until we came to a public campground. We'd be alone there, set up camp, and the next morning early, get in our ol' huntin' car, cross the creek, and start up the switchback road to about four thousand feet. You couldn't believe the scenery—and was that ever deer country. It was marvelous. It was a bad hunt if ya didn't get your buck in the first two hours of the season. Ya know, I downright admired the beautiful Cascades in the state of Washington.

Well, Brush Country doesn't have any apples except the prickly pear variety, and there's no Cascade Mountain Range here, and no one has yet driven out on Medina Lake to go ice fishing. Personally I don't care to go ice fishing on Medina Lake, and I can get an apple in season that may not go *crack* when ya bite into it. But the deer huntin' here is exciting, and ya don't have to mess with that twenty-five degrees below business. So I reckon I'd have to say that as good a place as the Evergreen State is, Texas and Brush Country is better.

Eatin' Humble Pie

Most of us *Homo sapiens* eventually find some activity in which we excel. Sometimes, though, we may not be as proficient in those activities as we might think, and we may not be capable of performing those activities exceptionally well on a consistent basis. Occasionally we might even think, *Well, I got that thing mastered, no sweat—nothing to it.* Then some later time, it becomes apparent that we haven't mastered that skill quite as well as we thought. That's been the way most things have been with me. Golf is a good example.

Back in 1961, I began playing golf down in Montgomery, Alabama. I played daily for six months, took a few lessons, practiced, and finally got to the point where on this beautiful late spring day, I came to the tee of the eighteenth hole with seventy-five strokes. All I had to do was par this one fairly short hole, and I'd finish with a seventy-nine—my first time ever to break eighty. Ya know, I'd mastered that game, nothing to it, just step up there, make sure your grip is okay, stance is just right, eye on the ball, slow backswing ... then something happened on the downswing, and that ol' ball took off with a huge curving slice to the left. Well, that was out of bounds, and to make a long story short, nine strokes later, I finally poked that crazy ball in the cup. I never came close to breaking eighty again, and not long after, I devoted my attention to other matters. But golf is a humbling experience for someone who thinks he's about got it mastered. You can ask any pro.

Landing airplanes is kinda like that, too—at least for me. About five thousand hours of my flying time was logged as an instructor pilot, and much of that time I spent in the traffic pattern teaching other pilots how to land four-engine airplane transports. Sometimes we'd log twenty or so landings in a four-hour training period. When you've been through thousands of landings, ya kinda like to think you're pretty good at it. But then there'll come one of those days when it's all just downright embarrassing. One time I was landing a C-141 at Amman, Jordan, and I had about twenty pilots on board in addition to the other one hundred or so passengers. Just after crossing the runway threshold, I started to flare in preparation for touchdown, and wow—that ol' bird simply quit flying. We crashed, bounced about twenty-five feet back in the air, and bounced again. It was the worst landing I ever made—terrible—and those pilots never let me forget it. Fortunately we were over the runway, and the landing gear was down, so the only damage was to my pride. I had another similar experience at Santa Monica, California.

Dove hunting can kinda be like golf and landing airplanes. A fella can get to the point where he thinks he's pretty good at hitting those grey, darting ghosts, but there'll always come a time when he finds out differently. The other day, Hartley Howard, Jerry Young, and I were out trying to bag a few ol' birds, and I did bag a few—very few. To be specific, I shot thirty-one times and killed seven birds. Last year on another bad day, I shot twenty-five times and picked up four birds. I don't know why those things happen. Maybe it has something to do with biorhythms, or maybe it has something to do with the Lord kinda keeping tabs and making certain that a person keeps the proper perspective. Personally, I think that's the answer. And when it happens, I get the message: eat humble pie and press on.

Corncob Fights and Swimmin' Holes

Back in the good ol' days, the kids here and in most other rural communities lived in a completely different environment than do today's youngsters. As the aftermath of the 1929 stock market crash unfolded, the Great Depression came down and in one fashion or another, touched practically every American. So in those days, most adults spent their time trying to earn a subsistence living for the family. Therefore, there were few—if any—supervised activities for young people.

In Devine in those times, there was no little league, Boy Scouts, Girl Scouts, eighth grade football—no nothing. If'n ya wanted to be entertained when you were a kid, ya kinda entertained yourself. There wasn't any TV. Parents didn't serve as taxi drivers constantly dropping off and picking up young folk. And if'n you was a young buck, you'd best not get caught downtown after school, 'cause the superintendent or principal might lay some heavy words on ya—at least he'd say, "Git," and he meant "git home." Ya didn't have any business downtown.

What we did to entertain ourselves no kid would think of doing today. But it really wasn't that difficult, because the only time most of us had for entertainment anyway was a few hours on Sunday afternoon. The rest of the time, if we weren't in school, we were workin'. But on a Sunday afternoon, the two swimming holes on Chacon creek would be filled with young 'uns. We carried our swimming suits with us—had 'em since birth—and after wading through those grass burrs and goat heads barefooted, we'd get to the swimming hole, peel, and dive in. Not long after everyone got in, we'd choose up sides and launch a full-scale mud fight. There ain't nothin' like getting hit right smack dab in the middle of the face with one o' them Chacon Creek black dirt and clay mud balls. I can still taste it. Sure, cows used that creek; there were snakes, eels, turtles, and no tellin' what else. But no matter—that was fun, and we survived.

Now if it was a little too cold to go swimming, we'd repair to the two-story barn out in the lot, choose up sides, and have a corncob fight. Now that was real fun. First, you assembled the gang—a couple Briscoes, six or seven Reduses, and eight or ten town kids. Then ya hauled ten or twelve bushels of corncobs outta the hog pen up to the loft for the side that was to defend the fort. Ya had to be selective in getting the right kind of cob. What ya wanted was one that had been mud-soaked and mostly—but not completely—dried out. It would be heavy and hard. It would also have a more accurate trajectory, and when ya got one o' them kinda cobs upside the head, it'd take a little hide with it when it ricocheted off. Well, anyway, when the guys were ready, we'd begin, and the battle raged until we became tired of that game or the fort guys played outta cobs. At any rate, we'd get our heads together and decide on what we were gonna do next. If'n it was fall, we'd probably play football.

Now our footballs seldom had air in them. Ya see, out in the country, one o' them air-filled types were short lived. Ya'd kick it into a prickly pear or mesquite tree, and that was all she wrote. We'd stuff that ol' football with newspaper, leave it outside in the elements, and you'd have an eight-pound football to throw around. Our playin' field was a packed dirt road—stone hard with gravel and rocks. We played tackle football with no pads, supervision, shoes, or much sense.

Well, those were just a few ways we entertained ourselves, and I'm not recommending we return to a time of unsupervised activities for young people. But I do think we sometimes get carried away with all these activities, and we need to be somewhat concerned that by planning and supervising every conceivable activity, we in some way reduce our young people's initiative and ingenuity—and those are two very important personal characteristics. So even though corncobs are hard to come by and the Chacon is even muddier than it used to be, there are still wholesome things young folks can do with a little creativity and resourcefulness.

DECEMBER 7, 1978

The Pioneers Who Wore Skirts

So often when we think of how this land was tamed, we think of the tamers—Bigfoot Wallace, Jack Hays, Tom Galbreath, Ben Highsmith, Kit Ackland, Ed Westfall, and others with such reputations. And this isn't to belittle the tremendous contributions they made, but there were those settlers who had given names unlike the Bens or Toms—more like Sarah or maybe Mary. Sure, the Sarahs and Marys didn't poke an ol' minnie ball down the gullet of a muzzle loader, mount up, and charge off into the wilderness after a bunch of Indians who'd just stolen all the family's horses. But don't think for a minute that the Sarahs and Marys didn't pay the price, because they did—and many made the supreme sacrifice. Consider Mrs. Sarah J. Kinchaloe and Mrs. Bowlin of Sabinal Canyon.

In 1866, the Kinchaloe family was living on Little Creek three miles northeast of what's now Utopia. The family consisted of the father, mother, and four young children; the oldest was eight and the youngest eight months. Although Sabinal Canyon had been settled since 1852 or so, it still remained sparsely settled in 1866. Anyway, early one morning, Mr. Kinchaloe and a neighbor, Mr. Bowlin, departed on a trip twelve miles up the canyon to obtain some corn. The men were to be gone overnight; therefore, the Bowlin family came to spend the night with the Kinchaloes. The frontier Kinchaloe home—like practically all other first-generation Brush Country frontier homes—was made of pickets with a grass roof. Really, the pickets were nothing more than posts placed in the ground like fence posts with one post being placed alongside the adjacent posts and mud placed in between the posts. Sometimes the mud fell out—as was the case in the Kinchaloe home—so there were some fairly wide cracks in the outside walls. In addition, there was a door at the rear of the house which could only be partially closed.

As darkness set in, the dogs became nervous and barked almost continuously—a sign in those times that Indians might be nearby. The ladies and their children made it almost through the night when the family sheepherder decided to go on a binge and broke into the house just before daybreak. Mrs. Kinchaloe obtained her rifle and routed him, and as he left, the dogs took after him and finally treed him on top of the smokehouse. There was no more trouble with him. But at daybreak, the ladies thought they'd best check on things over at the Bowlin home, and on arrival there, the Bowlin sheepherder also went into some kind of rage, and they had to tame him with the same rifle. After getting things straight there, the two pioneer ladies and their children returned to the Kinchaloe home.

As they approached the home, they observed two Indians running after the Kinchaloe horses. The families took refuge in the home, and when the Indians caught the horses, they mounted and came toward the home, unlatched the gate, and rode right into the yard. Mrs. Kinchaloe pointed the rifle at the Indians, and they ran to the rear of the house. She attempted to fire the rifle, but it didn't fire, and one of the Indians shouted "No buena" and then ran to the partially opened rear door and shot Mrs. Kindhaloe with an arrow. At practically the same time, the other Indian shoved a lance through a crack in the pickets and lanced her severely. The brave lady stood her ground, and after receiving eleven lance and arrow wounds, finally handed the rifle to Mrs. Bowlin and asked that she protect her children. Mrs. Kinchaloe could no longer stand. When she slumped to the floor, the Indians jumped into the house and fatally wounded Mrs. Bowlin with two arrows. The children were hidden under the bed, and the Indians, thinking both women were dead, took what they wanted from the home and left. As the Indians left, the children came from under the bed. The oldest, age nine, pulled arrows from Mrs. Kinchaloe and with one of the small Bowlin children hurried to the nearest neighbor some 2.5 miles distant. The neighbors quickly responded, and to shorten an already long story, Mrs. Kinchaloe survived and for years operated the Utopia Hotel.

So the next time ya think about the settlers or the pioneers, ya kinda want to remember that about half of them pioneers wore skirts. And many of those who wore skirts had more than a little to do with the taming of Brush Country.

Support Your Local Dynasty

I don't know how you feel about it, but a life with no excitement, no thrills, and no anticipation would be a mighty boring life. I mean, a person missing those important elements of life would be physically alive but emotionally dead. Of course, there are many ways to find excitement. For someone in a deer blind, the sight of a fourteen-point buck would kinda bring on the rigors. And for someone interested in flower gardens, a rose would be excitin'. For me, among other things, athletics kinda gets my emotions up on cloud nine. If ya haven't been to a Southwest Conference football game, ya oughta do that sometime, particularly when title contenders are playing. Even if there aren't contenders playing, it can be terribly exciting. This fall, my family attended the Baylor-A&M and Tech-Baylor games. Both stadiums were filled; almost fifty thousand were at each game. Wow! Excitement and electricity were in the air, bands were playin', flags were flyin', there were great cheers, and there was tremendous enthusiasm. And any Cowboy fan who has seen his team play would say the same. But ya know, ya don't need to attend a Southwest Conference or NFL game to get thrills in athletics. You can do that right here in Devine—really!

In sports, everyone recognizes the names Vince Lombardi, Bear Bryant, Tom Landry, and the like, because these folks have been successful in developing and coaching dynasties in either college or pro football. But Devine has its own sports dynasty in girls' high school basketball. Coach Gayle Sessions has a successful dynasty in common with aforementioned legends, but there the similarity stops. Ya see, Gayle is in a class by herself, and that class is considerably above those other noted personalities. All of those guys would love to have the record Gayle has. In the eleven years Gayle has been coach, how many championships do you think she has won? If you guessed eleven, you'd be right. In those eleven years, she has only lost three district games and won 270 games. Reckon any other team in any sport anywhere in the state of Texas could claim that kind of record? I doubt it.

This past weekend, the high school hosted the annual Christmas Tournament. And Saturday night, both the Warhorse and Arabians played in the finals. It was exciting! It was thrilling! If ya didn't attend, all isn't lost. The season is really just gettin' underway. But don't miss any more games. Get a schedule, and mark your calendar. It's fun. Ya might even see a coupla buddies, check on how many points their ol' bucks had, and cheer a lot for the Arabians and the Warhorses! This is your town, and a winning tradition in high school athletics does much to create a favorable community image. Come and support these student athletes and coaches at the tournament and home games; it's right good entertainment at a right good price.

1978 Was Different

Now, there ain't no other way of putting it. This was a weird crazy year. For the first six months, it didn't rain. Then one day in July, Bandera caught an average annual rainfall in just twenty-four hours. That storm was weird. It was too early for a tropical storm, but just all of a sudden, it kinda matured right here in Brush Country. Well then, things rocked along okay weather-wise; summer stretched right up to the second week in December. Then overnight, in comes an arctic freeze. It was crazy.

In the first half of 1978, quail didn't hatch as they should. Some say that for quail eggs to hatch, there must be moisture. Early in the year, there was little moisture available, and as a result, the quail crop was poor in 1978. Doves were real spotty, too. Some concentrations could be found, but they were few and far between—nothing like 1977, which was a banner year for dove hunters. I think there were two reasons for the poor dove crop. One, the local doves didn't hatch off very well, and two, it was so warm for so long that the northern doves didn't migrate until late. In November, there were droves of doves in the Ballinger area. And now, late in December, there are many doves here.

Crops didn't seem to fare too well, either. The corn wasn't up to par—we didn't get even one good roasting ear. The peaches were walnut-sized, and the maize crop hardly grew high enough to attract the grasshoppers. Even the mesquites were all messed up; usually by August, they take on a very dull appearance. This year, the mesquites were so green in early December that one would have thought it was spring.

Well, whatever caused all of these phenomena must have stirred up Southwest Conference football, too. Them ol' Aggies had a world-beater team. They crushed everybody till they went down to play Cougar High in Houston. Score at the half: Cougars 33, Aggies 0. Texas Tech had one of the nation's longest winning streaks going into the Arkansas game, where Arkansas led 42-0 at half. Baylor creamed Texas, Texas creamed Tech, and Tech creamed Baylor—weird. Arkansas creamed Tech, Tech beat Houston, and Houston bopped Arkansas.

Politics is always weird, but this year it was especially so. In November, Texas elected its first Republican governor in some one hundred years. Now I don't know what has caused all of this. The moon looks okay; its appearances are still predictable. There haven't been any recent atomic explosions. But whatever caused it, 1978 was different—but different doesn't necessarily mean bad. Taken in the total perspective—even in those times when things are a little weird—life in the Brush Country ain't too bad.

HB's family at their country retreat (Popalote) in 1997, blessed with the good life. L-R: Charli Eastburn Groen, Emalee Stewart Smith, Jarod Briscoe, Kate Briscoe Eastburn, Dillon Briscoe, Mary B Briscoe, Tess Outlaw, Erin Stewart, Taylor Eastburn, Henry Briscoe, Addison Outlaw, Ellee Stewart, Emily Briscoe, Colton Briscoe, Marianne Briscoe Outlaw, Mark Outlaw, Ben Briscoe

What about life in America? More people have a greater opportunity for the good life in America than any people in any country at any time anywhere in the world. Hopefully in 1979, we can concentrate less on the weird things and more on the real challenges: runaway inflation, soaring crime rates, and irresponsible leadership in some segments of government. Then just maybe, by this time next year, even more people will have an opportunity for the good life, and America will even be a greater place than it is now.

I hope that happens.

BRUSH COUNTRY BULL 1979

Marbles, Tops, and Washers

I feel sorry for today's young people. You see, today it's kinda difficult for a young person to be a kid. Our society will not let that happen. For one thing, a kid needs a swimmin' hole, and today there ain't many swimmin' holes, 'cause young folks mostly swim in concrete, chlorinated swimming pools—sometimes heated. In those pools, there's no mud to throw, no trees to dive from, no muddy banks to slide down, and no logs to float on. Gosh, a fella can't even run alongside a pool, so swimmin' in a pool can't be that much fun.

But that's only part of it. Can you believe growing up without ever playing marbles or tops or washers or even barb-a-ree? And of course, today's young girls have never heard of jacks or jumping rope. But back to marbles ... when spring came, so did marbles. Everything had its season—marbles, tops, even yo-yo's. In marble season, ya couldn't wait till recess to get out there on that rocky school ground, and ya quickly drew a pattern on the ground that appeared like an elongated football some two or three feet long; this was called the ring. Then everyone would put a marble or two in the ring. Some fifteen feet or so from the ring, you'd draw a line, and the players would tag for the first shot. Closest to the line would shoot first, then next closest would shoot, and so on. When shooting from the line, the pros would rainbow that old marble down there and try to lay up as close as they could to the marbles in the ring. The idea was to knock the marbles that had been placed in the ring outta there. As long as you continued to knock them out, you'd continue to shoot uninterrupted.

Some of the pros used agates for the shootin' traughs. A traugh was the word we used for the shootin' marble, and the marble in the ring was called the dredge. There would be marbles of all shapes and sizes made out of various materials from glass to metal. We could play marbles on the school grounds just as long as it wasn't for keeps. Mr. Willingham, the superintendent, didn't care much for those who played for keeps.

Now tops had their season too, and in season, everyone brought his top to school. If your top was a veteran of the top wars, it'd have a number of deep gouges where it'd been hit by other tops. A fella'd take a string 'bout three feet long, put a loop around the top's head, drop down to the spinner, and wind 'er up two-thirds of the way up from the spinner to the head. Then with a loop around your middle finger, turn the top upside down while holding it between your thumb and forefinger and let her rip. That ol' top would come down—I mean hummin' and dancin'. The harder ya threw it, the higher frequency the hum. Well, cascar was like keeps in marbles—it was taboo. The guys who played cascar would modify their tops, which would include a nail. They'd flat split your top in two.

Among other games, the girls played jacks and also jump rope. Boys also played jacks and did some rope-jumping. I did. Old-time jacks were made of metal, and there'd be maybe ten jacks in a set and a rubber ball. Toss that ball up in the air, and while it bounces no more than once, ya pick up one, then two, then three, and so on. Once you missed, then it would be the next person's turn. Now parents were real sensitive to jack season. A person would only have to walk across the floor barefooted once and step on a jack; after that, they'd be supersensitive.

In those days, most every kid played hide and seek and barb-a-ree. In downtown Devine, on a spring or fall night, ya could hear kids hollerin' "Barb-a-ree!" almost all over town. You could hear then, because after dark there was practically zero traffic—no noise pollution.

Well, young people will mature without marbles, tops, jacks, or jump rope, but they will have missed a lot by not experiencing those kinds of entertaining pastimes.

JANUARY 18, 1979

Dr. George Woods: A Fantastic Human Being

My *Funk and Wagnalls Dictionary* defines the word *saint* as "1) any Christian believer, 2) one of the blessed in heaven, 3) an angel, and finally 4) a very patient and unselfish person." I suppose those are accepted definitions, and if I had to identify one person I've known in my life who best fits the saint definition, the selection would be easy—simple. It wouldn't take three seconds, and the person I'd select would be endorsed by practically everyone who ever knew this man, and he is Dr. George S. Woods.

For those of you who are younger or have recently moved to this community, Dr. Woods was the only medical doctor in this community for years, and there simply aren't enough good adjectives to adequately describe him—patient, kind, gentle, warm, friendly, sympathetic. I can see and hear him now. He had a ruddy complexion, was slightly stoop-shouldered in his later years, had grey hair, and always wore a suit. He'd put his hand on my shoulder and say in a slow, soft Southern drawl, "Now, Henry, this is going to sting a little, but it won't be very bad." And somehow—even as a

Dr. George Woods

child—I knew it wouldn't be. I don't know how many trips I made to his office upstairs in the building immediately west of the Sears store, but in every case, I was always treated in the same courteous and kind way. I loved that man, and when I came home from college and the service, he always had time to sit and visit for a spell.

From the middle years on, my parents were in relatively poor health. Many times at two or three in the morning, I'd have to drive in to town, knock on Dr. Woods's door, and always get the same response. "Hurry back home, Henry, and tell your father (or mother) that I will be there in just a few minutes." He never failed. In 1937, my father had severe internal hemorrhaging and fainted late one might. As usual, Dr. Woods responded very promptly and determined that Dad's condition was so bad that he couldn't be moved to a hospital. For three months, Dad lay in bed. Under Dr. Woods's daily treatment, he finally regained his strength. Dr. Woods saved his life, and my family will never forget it.

After each house call, Dad would always ask, "What do I owe you, doctor?" The response was usually, "Uh, that'll be two dollars, George." I'm certain that many times, at many households, Dr. Woods never received two dollars. And I'm almost certain, too, that if he didn't see it, he probably said no more about it, because he knew that in mid-Depression, many couldn't pay for the treatment. He treated them anyway.

Dr. Woods also had a sense of humor. Back in about 1936 or so, he bought a new Ford coupe. One hot summer day, he drove Dad and another fella to Hondo. In those days, a car with a heater was unheard of. So as they were driving along, Dr. Woods reached down and turned on the heater. In a few minutes, all three were mopping their brows. Finally, Dr. Woods said, "It's a warm day, isn't it?"

"Warm ain't the word. It's flat out hot, and the longer we drive, the hotter it gets." Finally, in a few minutes, this fella shouted, "Stop this thing, Doc. She's burnin' up!" Dr. Woods used to enjoy telling that story.

Well, unlike some of those in the medical professional today, Dr. Woods didn't live in a great, huge, modern home, and he didn't own a great amount of property, either. He wouldn't have understood how some doctors have abused the Medicare payment system; he was cut of a different cloth. But ya know, Dr. Woods was surely one of the world's richest men, because he served his fellow man in a way that few people ever did. He was responsive, understanding, wonderful, delightful—an absolutely fantastic human being. It's too bad we didn't have the technological capability in those days to film how Dr. Woods interacted with his patients. Every medical school in the nation could have used him as an example for what an aspiring doctor's bedside manner should be.

Saturday Night at the Movies

Recently, San Antonio's Majestic Theater reopened, and much publicity was directed to that event. In its heyday, the Majestic provided a tremendous amount of entertainment for many San Antonio area residents. Back in the big movie days, many Devine folks spent leisure time there not only enjoying movies, but also the big bands. I've spent my share of time there, but San Antonio wasn't the only city with a Majestic. Ya see, Devine also had its Majestic which provided much entertainment.

Next door to Schott's Model Market and across the street from Winn's, the Majestic still stands, although not now so majestic as it once was. Often when passing there, I reflect on the Saturday nights of long ago. Saturday nights—even in mid-Depression—ya went to the Saturday night movie. And that means Westerns, and Westerns in those days meant Johnny MacBrown, Buck Jones, Hoot Gibson, Tom Mix, Gene Autrey, Roy Rogers, and other such types. Now in those days, movie makers paid little attention to technical aspects and sometimes strayed from the plot. In almost every movie, there'd be the white hatters against the black hatters or cowboys against the Indians, but regardless of who was pitted against whom, they could flat be in the middle of a horrendous gunfight when all of a sudden they'd draw up them steeds, gather together with a guitar and a coupla fiddles, and break out in song. After a song or two, they'd resume their fight.

Of course the setting for many of these Westerns would be Texas. They'd be coming in to Del Rio, and in the background, there'd be these huge mountains—snow-capped peaks and all. Funny, but I never could locate those peaks around Del Rio. Another thing about technical factors was that when a fella made ready to fire his six-gun, he'd raise the barrel to a vertical position and then sling it downward when ready to fire as if to throw the bullet outta the barrel. Those six-guns were something else, too; it wasn't uncommon for a fella to fire them ten or twelve times without reloading.

There were a few other aspects of those Westerns that were somewhat questionable. I mean, there weren't nary a Western made in those days that the hero wouldn't be up on the second floor of a two-story building (usually the town saloon), and he'd be in a tight spot. No sweat—he'd leap from on high, legs spread, and hit right smack dab in the middle of his saddle, which just happened to be on his horse, which just happened to have the reins back over its neck, ready to go. Another method often used to mount a horse in a hurry was to approach the horse from behind in a leapfrog fashion and land in the saddle. Finally, another way was to have the horse take off in a dead run and then the actor would grab the saddle horn and swing up into the saddle—very impressive.

Another strange thing about those ol' movies was that buggy wheels always ran backwards. Today, buggy wheels still run backwards, even though there have been some technical advances in the state of the art. But even more weird than that was back in the ol' days, dirt and dust weren't dirty. Really—take ol' Tom Mix; he never had a speck of dirt on his white hat, and his white neckerchief was always spotless, and so were Gene Autry's and Hoot's. They simply didn't get dirty.

Forgetting the technical aspects for a moment, in those days, a fella under twelve could get in to the movies for a dime. For that fee, you'd see the following: a newsreel with two pieces of week-old news, a comedy, a serial, previews of coming attractions, and finally the feature movie. Now the serial was a movie in itself, and each Saturday, there'd be ol' Buck Jones fighting it out with the black hatters. Everyone knew when the serial was about to end, because the hero would be in this fistfight with the black hat guy, and our hero would be just barely hanging on to some rocks before falling off this cliff. The bad guy would be stomping his knuckles, and it'd end for that week. You'd have to come next week to learn how the hero got hisself outta the fix. Those were the original cliffhangers.

One thing I liked about the old movies was that Gene or Roy would never hold a girl's hand, much less kiss her. We could use a return to something more entertaining than graphic depictions of folks in the sack. Overall, today's movies are quite a departure from the movies of old. On the plus side, today's movies have fantastic photography and make the most of all kinds of technical innovations. On the minus side, they offer too much gratuitous sex, use more foul than fair language, and have little to no plot. There are some exceptions, but few. For me, given a choice between the lousy movies of the Depression-era Westerns and today's lousy movies, I'd choose neither. To me, the great era of movie-making was the '40s, '50s, and '60s. In those years, movies were made without a tremendous amount of violence or pointless sex—no profanity, good photography, *and* a plot. What a great source of real entertainment. I'd like to see a return of that kind of movie. I might not view them with the allegiance I have for Hoot and his buddies back in the Depression days, but I'd appreciate having the option to see a great movie every now and then.

Memories Linger On

This hasn't much to do with the Brush Country, but some of you may find it interesting. For some ten years or so, I flew the ol' C-124 Globemaster. I loved that ol' plane but man, was it something else. In ten years, I know that at least 75 or more times one of the engines would fail in fight. And there were a coupla pretty serious fires and many "air-aborts" and late departures, etc. Sometimes, halfway out across the Pacific from California to Hawaii, the head winds would be too strong and we'd have to turn around and cone back. I hated that.

Another thing was that the worst altitudes to penetrate rough weather was from six thousand to ten thousand feet. That just happened to be the normal cruise altitude for the C-124 and the one place in the world having the worst flying weather is the North Atlantic. In the C-124, lovingly referred to as "Old Shakey," we'd sometimes be in terrible weather all the way from Newfoundland to England. Turbulence, shaking, ice, poor communication. Sometimes we weren't really sure of our position and at night, in that weather, you'd have static electricity build up and make strange patterns all over the windshield. At times, the electricity would be so heavy that it would discharge off the airplane with a brilliant lightning-like explosion. If you happened to be kinda drowsy, that explosion would instantly bring you back to your senses.

Anyway, that ol' plane's performance was affected by a number of factors. Runway elevation was important and so was the temperature. On a hot day in Denver (elevation about six thousand feet) you couldn't onload much because at that elevation the engines simply wouldn't perform. The takeoff criteria was that the plane had to be capable of climbing at 60 feet per minute on three engines, should one engine fail on takeoff. Shoot, I've seen times when Old Shakey wouldn't climb 50 feet per minute when all four engines were operating. But, Old Shakey was an impressive bird, each of its four engines developed, or were supposed to have developed, thirty-seven hundred horsepower. Sometimes those horses seemed to have distemper or sleeping sickness.

Rare shot of C-124s in formation, 1953.

A takeoff at night was an unforgettable experience for someone in the passenger compartment. First of all, the airplane was not insulated or pressurized and a passenger or crew member couldn't hear himself think. Secondly, at "maximum power" the exhaust collector rings would glow a bright cherry red and as power increased for takeoff, static electricity would build up on the prop tips and continue building as power was increased until it would flow like liquid fire back over the cowling and even down off the wing's trailing edge—some 20 feet away. Certainly, anyone who ever rode in Old Shakey's cabin for takeoff at night never forgot that experience.

In the mid-sixties, a great revolution took place. Old Shakey's time was about to end and it was being replaced by the C-141 Starlighter which had four big twenty thousand pound thrust fan-jet engines. What a change. The C-141 was, if anything, overpowered. On my first trip as a C-141 aircraft commander, I was taking off from Moffett Naval Air Station and San Francisco Bay's southern tip. With a 65,000 pound payload and a gross weight of over 300,000 pounds we were heading to Hawaii for a refueling stop, then on to Guam. Moffett has mountains to the east and west and had we been taking off in Old Shakey, we'd have had to climb straight ahead for a ways, then reverse course and climb northward over the Bay. When crossing over the Golden Gate Bridge, we'd turn out over the Pacific and set course for Hawaii. In the C-141, after take off, you'd retract the gear and flaps, and make a right turn directly towards the mountains, which at our speed of only 250 knots were only about two minutes away. But when climbing at four thousand feet per minute, when you got to the mountains, you'd be at least four thousand feet above them. Fantastic. In a few minutes, you'd be up at "flight level 350" or thirty-five thousand feet and setting sail for Hawaii.

A short time after that trip to Guam I was enroute to Madrid. Halfway across the Atlantic we lost oil pressure on one of the engines and had to shut it down. Then, we were still using regulations we used with Old Shakey and when in an emergency situation, over two hours from landfall, you requested an Air Rescue intercept, so we did. The Air Rescue airplane, a turboprop C-130 had to come from quite a distance south from Madrid. When we shut an engine down, we had to "drift down" from thirty nine thousand to thirty five thousand feet and the result was that at the lower altitude we had a stronger tailwind and our groundspeed increased to 550 knots. The Air Rescue "bird" intercepted us about 25 miles from Madrid. So that old procedure wasn't really valid anymore.

Well, I flew that ol' C-141 for about six years, then spent some time getting qualified in the C-5, but even so, you never lose the love you had for some of the old airplanes. Today, the only Old Shakeys left can be found in a few museums around the country. No more collector rings glowing red hot, no sound of those expanding disk brakes, which could be heard for over 3 miles when you were taxiing along the runway. Those days are gone forever. But, the memories linger on.

Best Friends

One of the best friends I ever had—the lifelong type—was a fella named Duane Newcomb. Most of his buddies called him Mex. Now ol' Mex and I lived on the same road east from Devine, and when school was in session, we often walked barefoot down that sandy lane now known as the Rossville Road. Mex, his brother, Don, and mother, Mrs. Tom Weiss, lived with the grandmother, Mrs. Newcomb. We became closer friends while playing in the sand, and by the time we were about twelve or thirteen, we hunted together. We were after them varmints every possible minute.

When deer season came, we'd load up the ol' Ford truck and head for the Ulrich ranch near Tarpley. We'd stay two or three days and walk a million miles. Sadly, we weren't always successful in bagging game, but we ate a lot of kerosene-soaked cookies, slept in some rain-drenched beds, and went back year after year. We thought there was nothin' more fun than that.

We also spent our share of time in the sand-jacks looking for an ol' mossy horn. One time, Mex, Don, and I pulled into our favorite parking spot right in the middle of a scrub oak grove, and Mex shouted, *"Buck!"* A fleeting shadow kinda circled around to the south. We bailed out of that truck and shot down about a half acre of brush, but that buck just kept on movin'. Another time we pulled into that same parking lot long before daylight, just waitin' for the sun to rise. All of a sudden, there was this horrendous crash right up next to the truck. It was thirty minutes before we had composure enough to speak or try and determine the source of that terrible racket. Well, it was nothing more than a forty-foot oak tree that fell right next to us. I've often wondered why that ol' oak fell at that particular time since there wasn't any wind, but it did, and it was one of those events a person doesn't soon forget.

Ol' Mex had that marvelous capacity to be at home with anyone. Mex probably had more close friends from people of all age groups than anyone who ever lived in this community. He was super-intelligent; he could have talked with Einstein—or on the other hand, he could have communicated with anyone who happened to be on the opposite end of the intelligence spectrum from Einstein. He was also one of the more talented musicians this area has ever produced. He played the clarinet in the University of Texas symphony. He was a masterful piano player and loved any kind of music—classical, country, or jazz.

Ol' Mex was also a master of the ridiculous. One time, he had taken a shotgun shell and replaced the shot with the inner workings of a pocket watch. Well, here comes this buzzard, and Mex said, "Watch this." That ol' buzzard wasn't more than twenty-five feet above us when Mex opened fire with this pocket watch load. It must have knocked that buzzard thirty feet higher, but he just kinda shook himself, lost a few feathers, and kept on flying. In about three seconds, there were springs, nuts, and bolts falling all around us.

Well, I'll always be glad for my lifelong friendship with Mex based on a wealth of mutual interests. And for those who knew Mex as I did, they'd all say that because of him, their days were a little more exciting, more pleasant, less serious, and far richer.

Mr. Johnnie

Unfortunately for America, the cooperative spirit and "service with a smile" philosophy so many of our citizens had for so long is on a drastic downturn. Cooperation and concern for others were probably carryovers from frontier days. The generation preceding mine was comprised of folks who believed in helping others. They believed in being nice to their neighbors. Back on the farm in the late twenties and early thirties, we had no electricity and therefore no refrigerator. And really, we didn't need one. Ya see, when your neighbor had roastin' ears, you had roastin' ears. Mostly in those days, you'd just happen to walk out on the front porch, and your neighbor would have left you a sack full of just right roastin' ears. The same thing was true with black-eyed peas, watermelons, cantaloupe, and tomatoes. If our neighbors had fresh vegetables, you had them, and usually ya didn't even have to pick them; they'd leave them right there on the porch. Now when hog-killin' time came and one of your neighbors killed a hog, here he'd come with a big chunk of pork. He didn't only bring you meat; he'd take some to all of the neighbors. Then when you and the other neighbors killed a hog, you'd share with others, too. You didn't need any refrigeration, 'cause you were friendly and generous with your neighbor.

In that generation was a man I'll never forget who bent over backward to help everyone, and without him, a lot of folks would have been in really bad shape during the Depression. His name was Johnnie Griffin. I called him Mr. Johnnie. Now Mr. Johnnie was the mail carrier out on RFD, and he was our mail carrier from the time I could remember until I left for college. In those days, there were no farm-to-market roads, and the only paved road in this part of the country was Highway 81. Everything else was dirt, which meant that six days a week, Mr. Johnnie drove some sixty or so miles on a dirt road (make that mud roads in wet weather). Mr. Johnnie would get through, no matter what the weather—even if the roads were impassable.

Mr. Johnnie was a kind and sympathetic man, service-oriented, and a concerned citizen at a time when there was a great need for people who cared. In the Depression, many farm folk had no car and no money to operate a car even if they had one. So whatta ya do if ya live ten miles from town and ya run outta one of the basic food staples? No sweat—ya just leave a note in the mailbox. "Mr. Jonnie, please bring me five pounds of sugar tomorrow. Thanks." Next day, a horn honks, and there's Mr. Johnnie with the mail and the sugar. He'd also have a smile and a few kind words, and he'd be gone.

If you wrote a letter and didn't have a stamp, just place the letter in the mail box with three cents, and Mr. Johnnie would buy you a stamp, lick it, and it's done. "Well, what was the charge for all that service?" Nothin'—just friends, service, concern, and people helpin' people.

You'd be out there shockin' hay, sweatin', plowin', herding cattle, or whatever, and you'd see this dust trail comin'. Here'd be Mister Johnnie, and no matter how far out you were from the road, look over there, and he'd be waving. Mr. Johnnie was a friendly guy.

Now before I cause all kinds of trouble for some of our rural carriers, there's no way today's carriers can provide that kind of service. It's impossible—illegal. Don't go getting any notion in your head, 'cause them days is gone forever. But I'll tell ya something ya might try. Be a little more like Mr. Johnnie: concerned, friendly, service-oriented, and helpful. I believe "friendly" is contagious, and besides that, by living like Mr. Johnnie did, there'd be more pride, more happiness, and considerably more self-satisfaction—really.

Goin' to Town: Visiting a Lost Art Today

During Depression days, come Saturday, most folks would simply quit working, take a bath, put on clean clothes (not necessarily better ones), and head to town. Usually ya didn't quit working until noon, though. And as soon after noon as everyone could get ready, you'd be off to the big city. Generally most folks came to town to buy what few staple foods they needed, but some also brought in a few eggs or maybe some chickens to sell. But probably the most important reason everyone came to town on Saturday was to visit—ya know, to find out what was happenin'. With no telephones in the country and no TV, radio, or daily newspaper, ya had to come to town to get updated.

Now those whose cars were equipped with current license plates would just drive right on down town and park—no problem. But if'n your old car didn't have current plates, well, you'd park back there under them oaks kinda behind Loggins and Lilly (the locker plant). Ya see, the street in front of Brown's Chevrolet and the locker plant was Highway 81, and ya wouldn't want to drive out on the highway without current plates. If'n ya lived west of town, you'd just kinda pull in there under them mesquite trees where the Devine Lumber Company is now located. Those who came in wagons and the ones on horseback would also use that area and the oaks behind Loggins and Lilly to tie up their teams or horses.

There were those folks who came and spent the entire day visiting, shopping, etc. Come noon, you'd see them back at their wagon, and it wasn't uncommon to see some ol' long legs hanging out the back while they was taking a little nap in preparation for more talk in the afternoon. Anyway, come about three in the afternoon, there in front of Adams Company (now Winns), ya usually couldn't find a place to sit, 'cause the spit-and-whittlers would have the sittin' places all took up. Across the street was a busy area, too—where State Farm is now located. There was a butcher shop. Then next to it (west) was the Post office; then came Mr. Penland's barber shop, which he operated with his son, Jud. I'll never forget that shop. It was one of my father's favorite hangouts, and I spent many an hour in there as a kid. I can see those two ol' pistols that used to hang in there—one a small four-barrel job with the grips missing from the handle and the other a large revolver of some make. As ya came in the door on the right, there was an advertisement poster that said "Friedman Shoes" and a green wooden bench with a large star drilled into it.

Downtown Devine, turn of the century.

Well anyway, on to the west was George Thompson's Texas Market, and then came the City Tailor Shop. Finally there was Howard Drug Store owned by Mr. David Howard. That was a place I loved. In town on a warm summer Saturday, I'd kinda whine, plead, beg, and cajole, and finally ol' Dad would come up with a nickel, and I'd be smoking over to the drug store's ice cream and Coke counter.

"Uh—give me one of them banana-nut ice cream bars, please." I'd fork over the nickel and then pray that when I finished with that ice cream and polished the stick, there'd be this one big word stenciled on it: *"Free."* If it were there, ya could go back and get another free. Fantastic—that was livin'! It didn't happen very often, but it did happen.

I don't really believe that those were the good ol' days, but at least in those times, people had time to talk and visit—and they enjoyed visiting. Visiting is a lost art today—almost unheard of. Ya show up over at a friend's house after dark, and he'll more than likely say, "Uh, what's the matter? Whattya need?" Anyway, that's something like the Depression days used to be. I don't reckon you'll ever see beautiful downtown Devine like that again—packed with wagons, horses, and spit-and-whittle groups. Things are different now—not necessarily better, but different.

Hammers, Handsaws, Axes, and Crosses

One of the big changes in lifestyle among Brush Country residents—and all over, for that matter—is a loss of skill in using hand tools. What I really mean to say is hand-powered tools. If you don't believe that's so, drop by some of the areas where houses are under construction and observe the tools being used. A plain ol' claw hammer is virtually unknown. Nowadays, an air-powered hammer is used with prepackaged nails, and the nails are fired into boards just as if one were firing a pistol. Now I reckon it doesn't take much skill to use an air hammer, but using a claw hammer is something else. For some reason, a hammer is one of the first tools that attracts a young 'un. He's got to have one when he starts building. But that boy will be long past twenty-one before he learns to use a claw hammer properly—if he ever learns. And in the learning process, there'll be many a bent nail, many a bruised finger or thumbnail, and too many nails will go zinging off through space from a poor hit. Two of the more common faults in using a hammer are not striking the nail head squarely with the hammer's face and choking up on the handle. Either of these could result in a missed hit, which could result in a string of unprintable words or a hammer thrown through a neighbor's window.

An ol' handsaw will also get a kid's attention at an early age; it's such a simple and useful tool. Anybody can use a handsaw properly— nothing to it. Well, anybody can use a handsaw, but few can do it right. Among the do-it-yourself types, I doubt that one in a thousand can use a handsaw and cut a board off "plumb." I still can't. I don't even try anymore, but there's plenty of real craftsmen who could and still can.

But practically all of those old tools required skill to use them correctly. And for some reason, they were appealing. Take an ol' crosscut saw. Get two guys who knew what there were doing, and they could zoom through a foot-thick log in no time. But it took time to learn to use a crosscut, and today there probably aren't five people in Medina County who could perform very well on the end of a crosscut. There's probably less than five who would want to use one. Still, a crosscut is something ya just have to try when ya see folks using one. But once you've tried it, ya kinda want to let someone else use it, 'cause it soon turns into work.

Way, way back in the day, there were drawknives, mortise axes, froes, and such. Those are long since part of a lost art. If ya happen to own some of those ol' tools, better hold onto them, 'cause they are valuable to collectors who have no intention of using them.

Finally, one of the most popular and useful tools in all of America's history is kinda going the way of others—the axe. If it hadn't been for the axe, I doubt America would have ever gotten off the ground. And the same thing could be said for the gun. With an axe and a gun, the pioneer "tamed" America—it's as simple as that. But try and find anyone under the age of thirty-five today who has any skill with an axe. They just aren't out there, because there isn't much need today for an axe. The chainsaws and bushwhackers have more or less taken up where the axe left off. To me, an axe has a kind of romance about it. Watch someone who knows how to use it, and you'll see those inch-thick chips flying' and hear the ring of that ol' blade when it bites deep into a log. If we had a national tool like we do for other things like birds and flowers, it oughta be the axe.

Well, the next time ya happen by a place where an older feller is using an axe, hammer, crosscut, or handsaw, you might stop and watch a bit, 'cause that sight's going the way of the horse-drawn carriage.

Poppin' Johnny

In 1937, my father bought our first tractor. It was a John Deere Poppin' Johnny—a two-cylinder job with absolutely no electrical system. That meant it had no lights—and worse, no starter. The thing ran on kerosene, but without a starter, you'd never get it started on kerosene, so it had a small tank which held about a gallon of gas. You attempted to start it with the fuel selector on the gas position. Then ya grabbed this flywheel that was conveniently configured with finger grips, and ya gave her a big tug, then another (and another and another), and finally, when ya were too tired to climb up on the tractor, it'd fire and begin that weird poppin' noise. After runnin' for a couple of minutes, you'd switch the fuel selector over to kerosene and then reach down between your knees and move the gear lever to reverse. Then ya push this elongated clutch lever forward, and you'd back up. Crazy—but that's the way it was.

I reckon that machine had about a twenty-five- or thirty-horse engine, but it had enough power to rear up on ya if'n ya happen to engage the clutch too fast when facing uphill. It also kinda reared up on ya if ya passed over one of them terraces at too high a speed. Anyway, I spent considerable time on that ol' tractor, and one of the first things I learned was that it had a very fine magneto. One day, Dad had me chopping some cockle burs, and they were big 'uns. I was pullin' this ol stalk-cutter with about six or so chopping blades on it. I was going along there, and this big, green leaf got wedged in between one of the sparkplugs and a metal cover that should have protected the plug. Well, at best, with the two cylinders working, that thing didn't sound too great, but then with only one cylinder percolatin', it really sounded terrible. So I immediately leaned forward and could see the leaf. I stopped the machine—but not the engine—dismounted, and just reached right in there and took hold of the ol' leaf. It really didn't take me long to let go of that leaf, 'cause that magneto kinda had me all charged up.

I don't mean to badmouth John Deere products; that ol' tractor was a mighty good machine, and for seven years or so, it was the only tractor we had. Unsophisticated as it was, ya couldn't compare it with the power sources we had before 1937. The pre-1937 power source was mule-driven (one cylinder). Ya had a heck of time trying to stay within the guides on each side—hands on the upper guides while attempting to keep the rows of peanuts exactly between the two plow points on either side. While you were concentrating on that, those mules would flat come to a dead stop if'n ya didn't slap them across the hind end with the reins every now and then. Sometimes they would respond to a "Get up there, mule," but not often. They soon learned to ignore most verbal commands. 'Course, they always responded to "Whoa" unless they were runnin' away. Then they wouldn't respond to anything. Well, ya come to the end of the row, and a couple of hours later, you'd be turned around and headed back down an adjacent row. It seemed to me that those ol' mules moved so slow when turning at the end of the row that you'd want to time them with a calendar. The one piece of equipment that was absolutely essential when cultivating was a little wire-constructed cage or muzzle that ya placed over each of the teams and supported from the top of his head. That kept him from eating the peanuts.

Well, when cultivatin' was through, a fella at least could ride. But when using an ol' hand plow, there wasn't any riding. Ya walked behind that ol' plow, a handle in each hand and the reins draped over your shoulder. There's no way that could be fun—walking behind that ol' hand plow, stepping on those clods, breaking the soil down there about two inches deep, and plowing a furrow no more than eight or ten inches. Ya needed your hands. In those days, one didn't hear the constant hum of tractor engines, but ya could hear an occasional "Git up there, mule."

The amazing thing was, though, that when using teams, there was a tremendous amount of produce grown right here in the Brush Country—corn, cotton, broomcorn, peanuts, watermelons, and cane. The corn was picked by hand and tossed in to a wagon; hay was cut with a mowing machine and raked and shocked right in the field and later hauled to a haystack, or if in rows, it might be cut by a row binder and put up in bundles. Mostly you'd stand those bundles up in shocks for a while before hauling them in to a big haystack. We did have balers in those days, but ya had to pull the baler up to a haystack or haul the shocks in to a baler. However ya did it, it wasn't much fun. Farming now is work, but then it was *really* work—I mean physical work. Sometimes—like now—ya didn't get much for what ya produced. But there is a certain attraction to farming, and there is a little bit of farmer in almost everyone. One of these days, the food we produce may be worth more than the oil the OPEC nations produce, and they might even need food as badly as we need the oil. When that happens, I'm sure they wouldn't mind paying $20 for a bushel of corn, regardless of whether the land was plowed by mule or Poppin' Johnny.

Early Warhorse Football

My first encounter with any kind of football was along about the time I was in the first grade. Some of my buddies had mentioned a game was going on, and it seemed as if a fella ought to check that out—and I did. As soon as school was out, I headed from the Green Alamo north up to that block where the Devine Public Library is now located. In those days, that's where the high school team played football. There were no stands, and I can well remember there were just a few folks standing there on the sidelines, and when I came on to the field about where the library is now, the game was already in progress. Games were played in the afternoon in those days. Anyway, I'll never forget my first glimpse of football. Standing as the deep back playing for the Devine Warhorses was no other than Wesley Thompson. He was a long, tall, skinny drink of water barking out those signals and waiting for the ball. I don't remember that Wesley was going to kick the ball, but I imagine that Devine ran out of the deep punt formation in those days. I do remember that as the years wore on, the football talk usually centered on whether Wesley was going to play again next year or not. The rules were not very stringent in those days, and for all I know, ol' Wesley might have been twenty-two or twenty-three years old before he finally dropped out of high school football.

Not long after that, the football games moved to an area that is now in between George's Garage and the railroad tracks. This field had a high board fence all the way around it, and the turf was mostly sand with plenty of sandburs to light on when tackled. So things kinda rocked on there for a while, and around 1935, there was a new field constructed right behind the high school that is now the Green Alamo. The lights were added somewhere along the mid-thirties, and many will remember the stands on the south side of the field. The stands probably ran all the way from the forty-yard line to the opposite forty and were some ten or so seats high. There were no stands on the north side.

There is only one way to describe the playing surface, and that was "gross." Generally the west end had a caliche turf which had just enough topsoil on it to grow a fine crop of goatheads. It was harder than most sedimentary rocks, and the hardness provided a fine supporting surface for the goatheads, which would be fully matured and totally hardened by September 1 when practice began. So when you were flying down that field and someone tackled ya from behind, you'd police up all the goatheads for eight or ten yards or so and simply grate all the hide off your elbows and head.

The bathhouse located on the east end of the field had its own interesting characteristics. It was single-wall construction with rusty sixteen-penny nails in place to hang your equipment. We practiced and played in the same equipment, and that includes socks that sometimes went the entire season without washing. After the first week or so, those ol' socks would just simply hang down loosely around your black high top shoes. Our pants were heavy ducking khaki-colored with no elastic. The jerseys were basically maroon and gold; most were at least several years old. For a while, Don Lawton Tilley and I played with the same number—twelve—and that made it confusing for everybody, including the refs. But they could tell us apart, because being second string, mine was a different style, and it had a lot more holes than Don Lawton's.

It's true we didn't play with anything like the Astroturf, tear-a-way jerseys, or lighted stadiums that today's young players enjoy. But ask any old-timer, and he'll tell you what a kick we got out of playing Devine Warhorse football in the 1930s and '40s.

Jawin' at the KKK

There where Mark Kidd's State Farm insurance is now located for years (1941–1960) was the Kozy Korner Kafe. The KKK was owned and operated by Travis and Peaches Sollock, and they were open from early morn till about milking time. A fella could get just about anything ya wanted to eat there, but mostly it was the town gatherin' place for the folks who liked to sit, drink coffee, and talk.

There have probably been more cattle trades, land sales, and other deals made there in the Kozy Korner than most anyplace around. Come election time, the news, rumors, and whatever ran hot and heavy all found their way to the KKK. If ya pulled in there about 8:30 a.m. in the summer, winter, or whenever back during the Big War, there'd already be one spot taken. Directly out in front, you'd see the tan 1937 Chevrolet sedan owned by none other than Biggie Hester. Now Biggie was a trader extraordinaire. He dealt in anything and everything—nothing too little or too large. He loved to trade, but he wasn't in it just for the fun of it. He knew his business, and he just about knew the market value of almost anything right down to the very penny. When trading, he'd have a newcomer or green-horn thinking, *Well, this is just a poor, ol', dumb country boy* when really, ol' Biggie was sly as a fox. Another frequent customer was Raymond Redus; he'd be readin' the newspaper and drinkin' coffee. Ol' Temple Adams (a cattle trader) would show up too sometime during the day along with Dib Whitfield and many others.

My father, George Briscoe, could be found there about 2:00 p.m. until a little before milking time. After school was out, some of the schoolteachers would head on down for a cup and a checkup on the latest local news.

In my teenage years, our daily newspaper was always left at the KKK, and on those rare afternoons when Dad didn't go in to get the paper, I'd stop by and pick it up. At that age, I didn't quite understand the society there, but I think now I'm beginning to understand it a little better. Just the other day, I had a cup with some ol' buddies. Let's see— there was Joe Stroud, Harlan Ontjes, and Lewis Bendle. That was a crowd! Ol' Harlan was sayin', "Them rattlesnakes down there below Bigfoot is some of the most dangerous snakes in the world."

George Briscoe, 1936, in the heyday of the Kozy Korner Kafe.

"Why's that, Harlan; don't they rattle?" Joe asks.

"Yeah, they rattle all right, but them snakes is so big and long that you can be standin' right next to their heads, and it's so far to their tails that ya can't hear them rattlin'!"

"Ya, I drove over one the other day, and it blew out my front tire!"

Yep, we were thick in it.

Well, ya sit there awhile and talk about big snakes, politics, fishing, cat-hunting, cars, gasoline prices, land sales, people, jalapeños, football, and the lack of or excess of rain. Then ya just have to say a few words about cattle prices and Jimmy Carter, too. I don't see much tension in those groups—no uptight feelings—just friendly, funny, and entertaining people. A fella can get all the local news without having to endure the commercials. So I reckon now I understand why Dad used to spend a coupla hours at the Kozy Korner Kafe almost every afternoon "pickin' up the paper." It's fun to sit there and jaw with your friends.

Redusville, USA

Going southeastward out of Devine and down FM 3176, you continue on past Independent Market. Then go up over the Interstate 35 overpass on past Tharron Savage's home on the right, and before you get to Raburn Cadenhead's, you'll see an area now overgrown in mesquites. Also on the right about 150 yards before Raburn's place, in the twenties, thirties, and later, there was a yellowish, square-shaped house kinda up close to the road. That one house and its residents were known to my generation as Redusville. Now you'll not find that name on a roadmap, and in those days, there was no road marker to advise a traveler about entering or leaving Redusville.

But the reason that one home was called Redusville was that the number of folks who resided there justified community status. To begin with, there was Clem and Hazel Redus, the parents there by date and rank. Then there was John C., Martha, Mildred, Sallie B., Jean, Mary Nell, Bill, George, Dewayne, Charlie, Joe Robb, Clifford, Jan, and finally Allen Ray. Now even though Martha, Joe Robb, Mary Nell, and Jack died in their youth, the number of folks living under that one roof was considerable.

I have a lot of fond memories about Redusville, and here are some of the most lasting impressions. We were neighbors and good friends. We often visited, and here's what an evening in Redusville was like. On arriving, your first impression there was that Redusville was a very active place. Out in the back, an intramural baseball game would be going on, and Clem would be playing, too—but not everyone was encouraged to play. There would be Bill, Charlie, and countless others who would be digging a cave. That cave was no small-time hole, either. During the day, many hands had been working on it, and it was almost room-sized. When the ball game was over, everyone would grab a slingshot, and we'd get into this dirt clod fight. We'd substitute a rock if there were not enough dirt clods to go around. When there were enough knotted heads, we'd report over to the haystacks and climb on them for a while. In those days, most folks would take an end piece of a two-inch pipe, stick it in the ground where it would stand up fifteen or twenty feet, and then stack hay around it. Mostly, parents wouldn't care too much for the kids playing on those haystacks. Sometimes there'd be five or ten haystacks standing right next to each other, and they kinda looked like a bunch of teepees. It was a fantastic place to play, and ol' George was the high wire artist. He had smooth wires strung between haystacks and would try to walk from one to the other, which also resulted in a knotted head.

Leaving the haystack, if there were still daylight enough, we'd go out on the gravel road running in front of the house, choose up sides, and play football with a paper-filled ball and play until it got dark or until skinned knees and elbows proved abundant. That would about complete an evening at Redusville.

Come summertime, what do you think they'd do with all those kids? The answer is: nothing. They'd do for themselves. It wasn't uncommon for them to head out en masse and on foot for the Bigfoot area arrowhead hunting. They'd be gone all day, exploring, checking out new territory, and looking for arrowheads. Sometimes they headed over in our direction. About nine or so, you'd look down there on the Chacon Creek Bridge, and there'd be the Redus kids. They'd be ready to go arrowhead hunting in the sand pits, and following that, have a mud fight and swim in the Chacon. We always joined them.

When school was in session, there wasn't any way Hazel could pack enough lunches for all those kids, and there was no feeding facility at the school, so there'd be Clem out there in front of what's now Green Alamo, parked along College Avenue and headed toward town. He'd be in his dark blue 1928 Ford Model A Touring car. For those who don't know, a touring car was nothing more than a two-seat convertible, and I don't ever recall seeing the top up on Clem's car. Anyway, when the bell rang to be let out for lunch, there'd be a great rush of kids headed for Redusville. The more senior of the kids took the front, and the younger ones took the back. Before they left, there would be a couple of them calling the roll to make certain everyone was on board for the trip home.

Well, today there is no mark there at Redusville, and there is no house or activity—just the sound of cars going by on the FM road and the wind blowing through the mesquites. And in a few years hence, there'll be no one around who ever knew that Redusville was a one-house town down south of Devine. But I seldom ever pass by there that I don't think of those ol' days and the good times we had in Redusville, USA.

Law 'n Order

One of the major social problems this country faces today is a lack of law enforcement. That lack cannot be attributed to the law enforcement officers but to the gutless liberal judges and a permissive attitude that pervades today's society. It hasn't been too many years back that America was fundamentally a law-abiding nation, and one reason that was so was because crime was controlled by the law enforcement officers. That was the case of Texas Ranger Captain Lee McNelly back in the 1870s.

In those times, there were many cattle rustlers down across the Rio Grande who made raid after raid across the river deep into the Texas interior. The governor soon responded to that situation by commissioning Captain McNelly to sign up a force of rangers and get after horse rustlers—and he did just that. He immediately signed some thirty rough and ready types and then took them into one of the better-equipped stores and bought each man a .50 Sharps—something akin to a hand-held cannon. It spoke with authority and had great range. Not long after he whipped his ranger force into shape, some raiders pushed far across the border, stole some cattle, broke into a store, and stole a number of fancy saddles. McNelly simply instructed his troops on how to indentify one of those saddles and then further informed his troops, "When ya see one o' them shady-looking characters a-ridin' in on one of them saddles, empty it!" In short order, it was no longer fashionable to ride in one of those saddles.

Not long after that incident, some twenty-odd rustlers had raided up the coast almost to Corpus and were driving a large herd of cattle down south. McNelly struck their trail and drove his men day and night until they caught up with them. The rustlers were alerted that the Rangers were inbound and took refuge in an oak grove. They were secure—they thought. But McNelly lined his men up and charged at breakneck speed right into that bunch, and the rustlers' defense simply crumpled—and so did fifteen of their men. McNelly had the Army unit at Brownville bring in the fifteen bodies and stack them there in the city square for all to see. It had an effect on would-be rustlers.

Well, you'd have to say McNelly was effective. But he wasn't the only lawman who operated in that fashion. Many served as judge, jury, defense, and executioner. Right here in Devine one Saturday afternoon long ago, I happened to witness this incident, which was interesting. This habitual troublemaker was at his old business of causing trouble. Someone called the law, and a lawman appeared on the scene and ordered the troublemaker to get out of his car. There was no response from the troublemaker—but many bad words. Quick as a cat, the lawman had the car door open and the troublemaker by the scuff of the neck, and they were off to jail—right down the middle of the street in a trot for everyone to see. Something about that sort of treatment has a sobering effect on troublemakers.

Come the 1960's, though, the pendulum swung the other way, and there was obviously some need for a swing. Some of those saddles that were emptied might have been good folks—could have been … probably weren't. We have swung so far in the opposite direction that there is practically no respect by the troublemakers and such ilk for our law enforcement officials. NcNelly and our old, efficient lawmen here in Devine wouldn't understand the way our law enforcement officers are exposed today. And I don't either. We certainly don't want to return to the off-the-cuff saddle-emptying days, but if we expect to have any respect for law and order, we better first have respect for the ones who serve to enforce the law. You can't have that respect if the officer doesn't have the authority. The current system isn't working. The thugs laugh at the enforcers, and sadly, they do far more than laugh. We need to swing that pendulum back more towards the center—no saddle-emptying, but no laughing thugs either. Everyone except the troublemakers and thugs will benefit.

A "Pre-Owned" 1933 Plymouth

In the year 1935 our ol' Model A Ford "done plumb wore out." So Dad was looking around for a somewhat later model auto than the faithful ol' Model A. This dude from down Pearsall way got word he was looking, so one summer afternoon he showed up with a "pre-owned" 1933 Plymouth four-door sedan. I can remember that afternoon like it was yesterday. It was a shiny black machine with a thin red stripe around it and red wheels. Apparently it appealed to Dad because he bought it. One of the biggest mistakes he ever made, but in no way could he have forecast how that car would turn out. It wouldn't be accurate to say that ol' car was a lemon. A "White Elephant" wouldn't do it justice either. There aren't words to describe what a sorry piece of equipment that pre-owned 1933 Plymouth was. I'm not saying that Plymouths were bad autos, but I am saying the one we had was totally terrible.

The first thing that went out was the brakes. I may be wrong about this, but the 1933 Plymouth may have been the first auto with hydraulic brakes. Before, most autos had mechanical brakes, a system of brake rods that connected to the brake pedal which, when activated, forced the brake shoes against the drums to stop the auto. But the ol' 33 had hydraulic brakes—some of the time. Most of the time it had nothing other than the force of gravity to bring it to a halt. The first time Mom drove that shiny new Plymouth we came cruising off the road, up the driveway, right in to the garage and on through the back of the garage with a horrendous crash. From that point on, the bottom portion of the garage's north wall was kinda "free floatin." You'd hit it with the bumper and it would fly up and then settle back down in its original place. Good arrangement.

Well, not long after that we made a trip to North Texas and

my parents took me out of school to go along. I'll never forget that trip. The only thing that the pioneers who traveled across the plains in the 1850's had to contend with, that we didn't, was that we weren't attacked by Indians. I mean, we launched outta the ol' driveway about four one morning and after three flats, four vaporlocks, ten overheats and two heart attacks, we pulled smartly in to a garage on the southern outskirts of Austin. It was straight up 10 am. Not too bad. We'd made 110 miles in 6 hours. Well, those garage folks did what they could and we were off again on the vaporlock, overheat, heart attack business until shortly before midnight when we pulled into downtown Dallas.

The return trip was a repeat agony, but Dad had persistence and held on to that bucket of bolts mainly because that was mid-Depression and there weren't many options. But, come winter, things got really interesting. As the cold weather came on, each morning was a repeat of the preceding morning.Dad, talented in many ways, had practically no mechanical aptitude. We'd finish milking, all the milk bottled and ready for delivery into town, the kids dressed for school, and we'd be off. Well, sorta off. The battery in the ol' Plymouth would turn over, but it wouldn't start. Someone would run get the horse, saddle him up, take a rope and tie him to the bumper and pull that lemon out of the garage backwards. Then Dad would pour boiling water on the engine. Reckon that was to heat it up. That wouldn't work. Then he'd get some hay and shucks or whatever and build a fire under the engine. That wouldn't work, either. We'd finally pull the thing backwards into the road, then tie the horse onto the front bumper and be off in a gallop. Eventually the thing would start, and backfire a few times. We'd untie the horse and Dad would sputter off in low gear like Barney Oldfield. He'd have her all revved up, kinda paying her back for being such a lousy machine. But there was no way you could properly "pay it back." Burning was too good for the Plymouth.

We got a few moments of revenge however. I remember one morning Dad was driving down this ol' wagon lane, where years of erosion and ruts lowered the road bed like a gulley with high banks on either side. The ol' Plymouth had a design flaw in that its rear doors opened forward. So, we were motatin' on down this wagon lane and the right rear door wasn't completely closed. One of us kids opened it slightly to slam it closed and that forward-opening door swung out a little, caught the bank on the right side and just kinda folded back against the rear fender. That was a sickening sound. With the folded right rear door and battered front bumper and grill from crashing into the garage, the shiny new 1933 Plymouth was soon not so shiny. Come the first broomcorn crop, Dad traded off that "frustration" for a 1935 Ford Sedan—but that's another story.

Great-Grandma

Up yonder in the Devine Evergreen Cemetery lies my great-grandmother, Mary A. Gray Scurlock Briscoe. She has one of the earliest birthdates of any buried there. She was born on Christmas day, 1820. She died here in Devine in 1910, and in the almost ninety years she lived, times were tough—real tough—for "Mammy," as the family affectionately called her.

Now the reason I bring the subject up is that each generation in America seems to have it easier than the preceding generation—at least, it appears that way. The danger in that circumstance is that one of these days, some of these generations ain't gonna be able to hack it. Take ol' Mammy, for example. Born back there in 1820 in Mississippi just south of Memphis, Tennessee, she married early in life. Not long after, her husband died—that's tough. Then along came this fella named ol' John Briscoe, and they up and got married on October 27, 1847. Now ol' John (my great-grandfather) didn't have it too easy either. He'd lost two previous wives. One died in Virginia and another in Tennessee. There was a minor age difference. Mammy was twenty-six, and John was fifty-three. I'm happy they were married, 'cause I wouldn't be here writin' this story had they decided the age difference was too great. In 1848, my grandfather, George T. Briscoe, was born, and not long thereafter, John Briscoe received a land grant of 444 acres for his participation in the War of 1812. The land was near Augusta, Arkansas, and the family then moved to the plantation.

At that time, John Briscoe owned some fifteen or so slaves, and the plantation prospered until the Civil War came. Then the Yankees came through the plantation and took everything—slaves, crops, cattle, money, everything. And in January of 1863, the family Bible records this event: "John Briscoe departed this life Jan. 3, 1863 in Arkansas on a bitter cold night of typhoid pneumonia." He was born in Virginia and fought in the War of 1812, having enlisted in the Pittsylvania courthouse. So there was Mammy—slaves, food, cattle all gone; oldest child was fourteen; and there were three other younger children. Things got rough. The story I heard many times was that if my grandfather had not been a good hunter, they would not have survived. The family hung tough for thirteen years, and in 1876, the plantation sold at public auction for $444.00, and they caught a boat down the White River on to New Orleans and finally Port Lavaca, Texas.

Mary Gray Briscoe, "Mammy."

For a while, they stayed at the Gray ranch near Port Lavaca, but in time, they came to Gonzales County. There the boys operated a mercantile store, and they were doing okay until it burned to the ground—tough again. They moved on and finally settled in Devine in 1883. I've heard my father, aunts, and uncles talk of Mammy—small little character, tough, knew how to cope with anything. Anyone having a problem would go to Mammy, and she would handle it. A person learns how to react and respond after years of coping. Mammy hung tough.

Now today, things don't look too bright out there on the horizon: the slowing economy, threats from other countries, the energy situation … and far too many soft children. When things get tough, they just lie down and roll up in a ball; they assume the possum posture. In Mammy's generation, people saw a way through hard times and obstacles; they persevered. We would do well as individuals and as a country to adopt Mammy's "hang tough" spirit.

Tongue, Turnip Greens, 'n Clabber

So far as I can determine, there is nothing on this earth that isn't subject to change, and I suppose that makes life interesting. One change that not many folks talk about—and some don't know about—is the change in the kinds of food we eat. And if you don't think there has been some tremendous change in that area, well, you probably aren't old enough to know what people not too long back thought was pretty fair grazin'.

Now let's say that you are a young buck and you come in after a hard day's work and you ask, "Uh, what's for supper?" No one says, "Let's go out for supper." The reply would be something like this: "We're going to have brains and turnip greens cooked with a slab of sowbelly, hominy, and for dessert, a bowl of cold clabber." Not too many years back, my dad would have been really excited about that menu. Brains I've never been too fond of, but cold clabber was hard to spit out. Ya take the skim milk and let it set up. Then put it in the ice box and get it real cold till it sorta resembles white Jell-O. Dish yourself a big bowl, and put some sugar on it—fantastic.

Many people eat cottage cheese today, but you may be surprised how the country folk used to make it. When the skim milk was in the set-up form, put it in a sugar sack and hang it on the clothesline to drip. After a few hours, you'd have some bona fide fresh cottage cheese.

When slaughtering a calf, you'd always save the sweetbreads (various organs). You couldn't beat chicken-fried sweetbreads, but the last time I ate some was about 1950. Now if you went to the meat department in a grocery store and asked for sweetbreads, they'd send you to the pastry aisle.

Ox tail and beef tongue were also common in those times.

Flying to Northern Canada one time, the crew and I stopped in for lunch at a diner, and I had the best food I've had anywhere, and the main course was beef tongue. I'll never forget it.

Other foods not so common anymore are pickled pig's feet, hog's head cheese, bone marrow, and there were those who ate rattlesnake, coons, armadillo, and other such varmints. You might have a hard time selling some of these foods these days to youngsters. But I say if you sit down to your supper tonight, you'd be mighty lucky if beef tongue, mustard greens, and cornbread were on the menu. I'd choose that over pizza anytime.

Goin' by "Air"

In the more than four years I spent in Lubbock at Texas Tech, I made some twenty-five round trips from home to school and back. All but about three of those were by "air," or "Air you going my way?" I was a veteran hitchhiker. And those were some real experiences. Now Devine to Lubbock is a fer piece—about 450 miles. On an average trip, you'd have to hitch seven or eight rides. Sometimes you'd not be so lucky, and it might take twelve rides or so. Just once, I caught a ride all the way from Lubbock to San Antone. That was unbelievable. Well, how come ya decided to hitchhike? Simple—there wasn't an alternative. I didn't have a car and didn't have enough money to ride the bus. But hitchhikin' could be exciting. It was also frustrating and cold—and even dangerous.

One of the more fun things about it was the people. Ya met all kinds of folks. In those days, it was relatively safe to pick up a hitchhiker, and if ya were a reasonably-dressed kid with a crew cut out there on the road with a big double T (Texas Tech) on his bag—well, ya usually didn't have to wait very long. Night was a different story, though, and I'll never forget one of my first experiences coming southbound out of Big Springs. This fella pulled up in a new machine, and I asked the usual first question—"How far ya going?"

"All the way." That should have been my first clue that something wasn't right, but I climbed in, and we were off. In thirty seconds we were doing over ninety, and in other thirty seconds, we were down around fifteen—just poking. I kinda looked at that dude, because we hadn't had time to say much. About that time, a fifteen-year-old, broken-down wreck passed us, and this fella says, "See them new Oldsmobiles; there ain't no way a fella can catch one o' them things." Right away, I perceived that this guy wasn't just under the influence. He was dead drunk. Anyway, he proceeded to floorboard that machine to try and catch that "new Olds," which was probably doing about 37 mph. Again, in a few seconds, we were up over ninety, and we passed that Terroplane like he was standing still. Just after passing, he came screeching off the shoulder and turned onto a dirt road to let me out. And that's a gasser. Out in the country, hitchhiking at night ain't no way to go. But I was ready to leave that dude and happy to get out alive.

HB, Texas Tech senior, 1952.

One Sunday afternoon late—this time northbound—a fella in a pickup dropped me off about ten miles south of Slayton, Texas, and I must have stayed there for four hours. No one would stop. Finally this ol' guy came along on a John Deere tractor, pulling a big plow. He stops and says, "I'm going all the way into Slayton. It'll take a while, but I think I'll make it. Want a ride?" So I put my bag up on that plow and climbed up next to it, and we were off to Slayton.

Worst of all was another Sunday morning outside Austin—terrible. I waited, thumbed, and grinned but couldn't get anyone to stop. Finally, this ol' Spanish-American War veteran came along in a Model A Ford roadster. He was riding shotgun, and a somewhat retarded kid was in the driver's seat. They'd been fishing and were headed for Brownwood, which was in the direction I was going. So I pitched my bag in the rumble seat and climbed in beside it. About a mile down the road, they came to a dead stop and took the front seat out, and the ol' veteran pulled out a hot beer and sucked on that for a while. From that point on, we stopped every ten or fifteen miles, and he'd repeat the procedure. The retarded kid and I continued on, averaging about nineteen knots groundspeed. Soon the ol' veteran began to sing, "She's My Filipino Baby." He continued that refrain almost all the way to Brownwood. I reckon he'd have sung it all the way except that ten miles out of Brownwood, he passed out.

Another time, a buddy and I were out northwest of San Antone. It was cold and rainy goin' back to Lubbocktown. Along comes this new Buick, and he's going to Tulia on the far side of Lubbock—fantastic! Northwest bound for an hour or so, we were following this new Olds, and after topping a hill, we saw a wreck down in the valley—a pickup truck on one side, a school bus on the other. It happened hours before. No one was around, but of course, the Olds was—as usual—in front of us. We were cruising on down the hill at about sixty per when at a distance of maybe seventy-five feet, we all realized at the same time that the Olds had stopped dead still smack dab in the center of the road. Our driver only had time to say, *"Ahhhhh!"* as we plowed head-on into the Olds's rear at 60 mph. I want to tell ya, there were a number of stretched necks in that Olds as they were suddenly launched northwest. We came to an immediate stop. My buddy was sitting in the back, covered with this fella's groceries, including eggs, molasses, and corn meal. He was a mess. But we survived with a few bruises. We set out on the road again, thumbs out, when an afternoon frog-strangler washed the last of the groceries off my friend. Finally, we hitched a ride in the back of a refrigerated grocery truck headed to Fredericksburg. As I said, that was a cool ride.

Well, young folks today won't have many hitchhiking experiences—and really, they might be better folks for it. But I wouldn't take anything for my hitchhiking adventures.

Bird Navigation

I don't know if you've ever thought about this or not—or even care, for that matter—but ya take a little ol' hummin' bird and watch that critter and begin to wonder about him. Come fall, he's gonna head south with many other birds, and from what I've heard, he goes way south—clean down into South America—to spend the winter. Next spring, come about March 19, he'll be back here in Brush Country. Barn swallows, of course, do the same thing, and I know that this spring, there were these swallows that came back to the precise same spot where they had a nest last year. They were perched there where I'd torn it down last winter. Then there are these small birds that migrate all the way from Alaska to Tierra Del Fuego, the southern-most point of South America. That's a long haul. And finally, there's the ol' gooney bird who launches out of Midway Island out near Hawaii and is gone for five or six months out to sea and then returns not only to the same small island, but also to the precise spot where it nested—weird. How in the world do those small creatures (well, the gooney bird isn't small) with even smaller brains navigate thousands of miles and return months later to the same nest?

The *Smithsonian* magazine this month has an article on that question, and it's very interesting. It starts out by discussing some tests with homing pigeons. Now if there is one bird that has highly sophisticated navigational abilities, it is the homing pigeon. I remember years ago, sitting in Memorial Stadium in Austin near the end of a football game, there would be dozens of homing pigeons released so they could carry the news, film, or whatever back to the newspaper as quickly as possible. Homing pigeons were used often in war—like WWI—for rapid communications. Amazingly, ya can release a homing pigeon almost anywhere within a few hundred miles of his home, and in practically no time, he'll be back home. But the *Smithsonian* found that there are certain locations around the world where the homing pigeon can't navigate. Jersey Hill, New York is one of those places. Release an ol' homing pigeon there; the bird takes off and seems to get oriented on course, and then all of a sudden, his navigation computers go haywire, and he becomes disoriented and often returns to the launching place, totally confused. Thus far, *Smithsonian* doesn't have an answer for why the pigeon can't navigate there, but they are studying the situation.

Scientists have discovered some amazing things about bird navigation. Birds seem to have a compass component and a map component. The compass component permits the bird to fly a straight line course in a particular direction. In order to navigate, the bird must have a map component, which enables the bird to identify certain objects along the route. At times, those objects might be the sun or stars, which means the birds use stars to navigate. Birds use celestial navigation? It's true. And sometimes those birds fly over two thousand miles nonstop over water. I mean, little birds do that, and ya know something else—scientists have determined that some of those small birds have an ability to determine what the weather situation is on the routes. If the weather is bad, they don't fly.

Now this is interesting, but one of the major advantages of studying something of this nature is to try to develop mechanical navigational equipment that would be as small and as effective as a hummingbird brain.

If that were possible, then all the weight required for multiple backup navigation systems on airplanes could be reduced tremendously. But other than that, just to know a little more about the wonders of God's creatures is fascinating.

What Is a Good Man?

Y ou've all heard someone describe another person as a "good man." Back in my father's generation and his father's generation, there were quite a few good men around, and there still are today. A good man was honest. When ya traded with a good man and he looked you square in the eye, shook your hand with a firm fist, and said, "I'll give you my word on it," that was it. You didn't need a contract or lawyers. His word was as good as gold.

Back in the olden days, a good man was a hard worker. The more time ya put in, the more sweat ya put out. And the more ya got done, the better fella you were. But I mean when you started a job, you got after it no matter what the temperature, humidity, rain, or other various circumstances. You finished the job. A good man didn't need much help or supervision.

A good man met his commitments—even the little ones. I used to have an ol' buddy up in Moses Lake, Washington by the name of Willie Burton. Willie and I used to fly, hunt, and fish together. When Willie told you he was going to do something, he did it. If he said "Hank, I'll be at your place at 5:15 in the morning," he didn't mean 5:16 or 5:30. We must have gone hunting and fishing a hundred times, and he was never once late. About ten seconds before arrival time, I'd look out the door, and there would be his 1951 Chevy turnin' the corner. He could be counted on, and he was that way about everything. Willie was and still is a good man.

A good man doesn't have many excuses. He doesn't need many. Back in the days when I went through aviation Cadet training, we were taught to reply to a senior officer in this way: "Yes, sir," "No, sir," or "No excuse, sir." You used whichever response was appropriate. In those days, they didn't want a bunch of lily-livered dudes walking around making excuses for every bad thing that happened. A good man won't rely on excuses for failure, and he won't often fail.

A good man is persistent. He'll hang tough and stick to it. He doesn't give up. He follows the old, well-known philosophy of "if at first you don't succeed; try, try again." He doesn't watch the clock or quit if things get tough. A good man will grit his teeth and say, "Press on."

A good man will be compassionate. He'll want to help his fellow man. When his neighbor needs him, the good man will be there, and he'll stay as long as he's needed. And he wouldn't think of accepting anything for his services.

A good man will have a solid relationship with God. And because of this relationship, a good man will possess all of the personal characteristics already mentioned, plus many others, including integrity, honor, humility, love, and patriotism. Well, that's a little bit of what it takes to be a good man. This country has had plenty of good men. Once we lose the capacity to turn out good men, ya might as well forget it—we ain't long for this world. Sometimes the "me generation" concerns me in that we have too many who follow the "if at first you don't succeed, *quit*" philosophy. For anyone who might be tempted to join them, here's a poem I copied from an old book that has been in my family for over a hundred years. Each one of our kids was given a framed copy of this poem when they left for college.

"It never pays to fret or growl when fortune seems your foe,
The better bred will push ahead and strike the braver blow.
For luck is work, and those who shirk should not lament their doom,
But yield the play and clear the way that better men have room."

Vietnam and Me: The Way it Was

You know, every war is different, and the reason that's so is because weapons constantly change—and changes in weapons mean that tactics and techniques must also change. Then too, the politicians are involved, and they place limitations on what their armed forces can and can't do. And that's the way it should be. But just think how the character of war has changed down through the ages. Alexander the Great was tremendously successful because he increased the length of the pike. When guns finally came along, men marched into battle in bright uniforms with bands playing. They formed long lines facing each other. The first line would fire, then kneel. Then the second line would fire and kneel, then the third, etc. They knelt to reload those ol' muzzleloaders. Then we advanced to gas, tanks, helicopters, and nuclear weapons. Now we've arrived at the point in warfare where we don't intend to win—weird. But all that kinda reminds me of *my* war—the Vietnam War.

Being a Vietnam veteran isn't much of an endorsement for anyone. Vietnam was a very unpopular war, and sometimes the veteran of that war doesn't have such a good feeling about it. I don't know how it was with you and your war, but here is the way it was with me in mine. One major difference might have been that I didn't experience the degree of danger that you did. Many Vietnam vets did experience danger, and many lost their lives there. But for me, the ten months I spent there were almost enjoyable. I was commander of a unit with only about eighty men. Our job was to meet, service, and maintain all of the Air Force and commercial transport aircraft that came in to DaNang. My boss was in Hawaii, and in ten months, he was there only once. It's always nice to have your boss four thousand miles away. I couldn't really hide, though, because we sent our reports daily, and he could tell from those reports if I was getting the job done or not. At DaNang, ya didn't go off base. Not many *wanted* to go off base. It was a grim place, and you weren't likely to encounter many friends there.

One thing I remember most about DaNang was the constant roar. The base was long and narrow, constructed alongside the two parallel runways. F-4s were taking off and landing around the clock, and the F-4 is a noisy airplane. Also, the Viet Cong held sway around there, and they wanted to make certain you didn't forget you were in a war zone. So three or four times a week, they'd fire 122 MM rockets in to the base. Sometimes they'd only fire four or five times, sometimes forty or fifty. They always fired between midnight and 4:00 a.m., because they had to carry their rockets to within six miles of the base. This couldn't be done until after dark. By the time they got the rockets set up, it would be after midnight. Anyway, just west of DaNang was Freedom Hill, and we had folks up there watching. When the VC fired their rockets, our watchers could see the ignition and would sound an alert siren down on the base. When the siren sounded, ya had about six seconds to take cover. Another officer and I shared a trailer which had sandbags placed about four feet high all around it. So when the siren sounded, all you could do was simply roll out of bed, grab your flak vest, put on your helmet, and pull your mattress over you. Then you kinda prayed that there wouldn't be a direct hit on the trailer. In short order, I got to where I could do all of this in about four seconds, and that left two seconds to pray. The rockets were fired in one salvo so they'd all impact within a span of four or five seconds, and that'd be it for that night. Then you could get up, put your mattress back on the bed, and sack out again.

But the nice thing about being over there for a while was the freedom I had. There weren't any household responsibilities. I didn't have to mow the lawn, wash the car, or anything like that after getting home from work. So every night, I'd play racquetball for three hours—super. On Saturdays and Sunday afternoons, we would play tennis and racquetball—not a bad way to fight a war.

But a coupla times when I was over there, I'd get this call from a two-star general in California, and he'd say, "Hey, Dad, I'd like for you to take some of your men and go down to Pleiju and run an airlift for three or four days."

"Aye-Aye, sir." That Pleiku was a wild place. Problem was that down there, the VC weren't so considerate. They'd fire rockets at you all day long and during the night, too. Like DaNang, the base was tremendously noisy in the daytime. At night, it was quiet. But we were hauling munitions into Pleiku for Vietnam Army Rangers getting outta there to Bien Hoa. At one time, we had over a half-million pounds of bombs and ammunition sitting there on the ramp. And while we were waiting for another airplane, we'd be sitting on the ammo boxes, and all of a sudden, this rocket would blow something up not too far off, and that would kinda unnerve ya—no warning, no nothing. At night, it was worse. You could hear them fire those rockets when it's quiet. You'd hear this *varrom*, and everyone would yell, *"Inbound!"* You'd hug that concrete floor as tightly as you could, and there would be this big explosion. That got kinda tiresome. Anyway, after three or four days, we'd finish the airlift, load our gear in a plane, and head on back to beautiful DaNang, which wasn't too beautiful.

In DaNang, most of my time was spent out on the flight line, and during the course of any day, it was excitin'. Three or four times daily, all of the crash equipment would dash out to the runway. That meant that probably an F-4 was coming in with battle damage, and I would position my Dodge pickup to watch the recovery. Every now and then, the jolly green giant (helicopters) would be successful and rescue a downed pilot. The pilot's outfit would always put on a tremendous reception. That went on all the time.

Recreation programs there were great—libraries, intramural sports, radio and TV, clubs, hobby shops, and a good BX, or base exchange. And the food wasn't that bad. But that was the way it was with me at DaNang. Talk to some of the troops out in the jungles, and ya get a totally different story—terrible conditions.

HB's squadron bids him farewell, Vietnam 1972.
The mustache also departed, never to return.

Well, I hope that's the last war America will be in involved in. But if we intend to remain free, it won't be. I believe if you're gonna get into a real, bona fide shootin' war, you oughta let it all hang out and get in there and win—the quicker, the better. It is terrible that fifty thousand Americans lost their lives fighting what some people thought was a no-win war. (But in one sense, we did fulfill our mission of containment; to bottle up the enemy so that communism wouldn't spread throughout southeast Asia. We completed that mission and left as programmed.)

For about six years, I flew wounded out of Vietnam back to the good ol' USA. On more than one occasion, some of those guys died while we were en route back to the states. They didn't make it. I spent a lot of time back there in the cabin talking with them. We usually carried about eighty half-litter cases, and half would be ambulatory. Few were bitter. Many hated the VC. Some had mixed emotions. They wanted to go back to their units but were also happy to be going home. But universally, they all responded in the same way when we touched ground in America. There would be a great cheer—yelling—the instant we touched down. That's what it's like for an American to be back home. You could hear them even up in the cockpit. Different, isn't it—different from the communist countries. People from those countries yell and cheer when they are able to leave and break the bondage. It's quite a contrast.

The following is an excerpt from a letter HB wrote home from Vietnam dated May 8, 1972: "This morning, while I was waiting at the landing strip for my next plane, the Jolly Greens came in in formation. Two Jolly Greens and two of the old WWII AIE-Sandys, which meant they had a successful mission. They had picked up these two Marine pilots; I drove around to watch the celebration. Let me tell you, those were two happy Marine pilots. They had been shot down in their F-4s and bailed out in country held by the Viet Cong. Jolly Greens got them out; they all were hosed down by these big water hoses and then the crews and the guys rescued had bottles of cold champagne waiting for them. They were turning up that champagne and swigging—you never saw two happier guys. One doesn't look forward to spending any time in the Hanoi Hilton. So, that is an escape from a pretty bad fate, for which they were mighty grateful. I know that the helo crews are very rewarded when they make a pick up like that."

Ol' Ray

In my early years, the one person I was closest to—other than immediate family members—was a fella name Reyes Jaramillo. Ray, we called him. Ray was about twelve years my senior, and early in life, he was orphaned. After he was orphaned, he was more or less adopted by the parents of Ralph and Frank Jaramillo. But when still in his teens, he began working for my father and continued with us for many years. I'll never forget ol' Ray, and many times when I pass through the Snyder, Post, and Justiceburg area of West Texas, I stop and try to locate him, since that's where he settled after leaving Devine. One of these days, I'm gonna find ol' Ray, 'cause now I know where he is. But anyway …

That Ray was something else. I couldn't say enough good about that guy—loyal, honest, hardworking, talented, great sense of humor, and could cope with almost any situation. Ray was about five foot seven and weighed about 135 pounds—a wiry sort of a guy with curly hair and a perpetual grin on his face. Need to overhaul an engine? Ray could do it. In those Depression days, with money scarce, ol' Ray could locate trouble with any piece of mechanical equipment and fix it. He could operate any kind of equipment. When the windmills needed pulling, Ray could do that. And when it came milking time at 5:00 a.m. and again before dark, Ray was there, milking his and someone else's share of the cows. Saddle up those horses and move a bunch of cows down to another place? Ray'd be there, and he could ride with the best. When it was a slack period and we kids would be playing marbles or a game of softball, Ray'd take his turn at that, too. Whether it was rabbit hunting, fishing, or whatever, he'd be ready. Late in the afternoon, quiet, just the milk hitting those ol' pails out there in the milk house, and there'd be this tremendous harmony:

Ray, his half-brother, Joe Hernandez, Juan, and Julio Zavala, going at it—some singing, some whistling, all in tune. At night in the summertime, old Ray on the fiddle and Joe on the guitar was great. Suffice it to say, ol' Ray could do anything well.

The one known picture of Ray Jaramillo, right, with George Briscoe during a flooding of the Chacon creek, 1953.

In the late '30s, my father became very ill at a time when Ray and his family were in West Texas picking cotton. Since we had a dairy and needed help, my mother wrote him a letter. Ray was home within twelve hours from the time he received that letter. *Loyal* isn't a strong enough word when describing ol' Ray Jaramillo. For all that loyalty, Ray was paid about $0.50 a day, six days a week—not much. But my father didn't have much, either. We delivered milk to the doorstep in Devine—$0.07 a quart—and even at that price, some didn't pay. Others would keep the milk bottles, and even more couldn't even think about buying milk at such a terrible price. Times were tough—real tough. But Ray also had a fair house, milk twice daily for his family, a garden plot, and chickens.

Come the mid-forties, and Ray decided that rather than go back and forth to West Texas each year, he'd simply stay there. I couldn't believe he'd actually go after all of those years we'd been together. All my life, Ray had been there with us for most of every year. He and my father had a fine relationship. If they ever had any kind of an argument, I never knew it. But I kinda remember Ray saying, "Out in West Texas, Mexican people are treated better." He wanted his children to have a better opportunity than he had had. I didn't understand then what he was saying, but as I grew older, I understood his feeling and concern. In those days, there was racial discrimination here—and discrimination all over America, for that matter.

For the past twenty years, this nation has undergone tremendous social turmoil in attempting to right wrongs that needed righting. In other words, our lifestyle in America and our moral obligations needed to line up with the Constitution. Today, though, there is still some discrimination—and reverse discrimination. So long as there are human beings on this earth, there will probably always be discrimination. But in this county, tremendous strides have been made toward enabling every citizen to have an opportunity and for all to have the God-given rights of life, liberty, and the pursuit of happiness. We're still working at being better in this regard.

Now it's time I think to kinda stand up, shake ourselves a mite, and get on with correcting some of the other major problems that face this nation. We can't realistically solve an injustice perpetrated on an Indian tribe in Maine in the mid-1700s by granting the few remaining descendants over in million acres of land in Maine. That's ridiculous—absurd. Only in Washington would anyone ever think of such a thing. So we'd best divert our attention to the fact that now less than 20 percent of the people in this world live in a free society. And that number is decreasing every day. That's important. We need to unite and be concerned about crime, justice, and energy and give those items great priority. If I could find ol' Ray, I know he'd say, "Yeah, let's get on with it. Life may have been tough in those ol' days, but it's better now, and I don't want to live under them Russians—so *vamanos.*"

Take to the Hills in the Fall

The first home of our married life was situated just east of Tokyo, Japan. The scenery out our modest front door was majestic with Mt. Fujiyama in full view. I'd take a gander at that snow-capped, twelve thousand-foot mountain in the early fall and get an itch to shoulder my musket and head to the hills. As a hunter, I was lucky in those early years, because later, when we lived in Tacoma, Washington, the awesome fourteen thousand-foot Mt. Rainier was a scant eighteen miles in the distance. You could almost see the aspens turning brilliant yellow when the snow began to pile up on the peaks. I couldn't wait to get up there in the hills on those cold, crisp mornings in mid-October for deer season and then in November for the elk season.

Later in my military career, we lived in Virginia, and there's nothing like the fall season up east. Words can't describe the beauty of it all. In the Washington, DC area about mid-October, the maples, beech, and oaks are all in full color. If you drive due west, the first mountain range is the Blue Ridge, home of Skyline Drive, surely the most beautiful sixty-five miles of earth at that time of year. The next range west—the Appalachian Wilderness—offers a primitive hunting season in mid-October that includes muzzleloaders and bow hunting.

Out there before the crack of dawn, ya shoulder your ol' musket after pouring a little powder down the barrel, rammin' a ball down the tube, and securing a percussion cap on the nipple. Then, with a sandwich or two, ya light a shuck on out to the hills. Ya head out through the woods slowly, looking, listening, and smellin'. If'n your lucky, you *won't* see an ol' buck. 'Cause when ya see a buck and bring him down, the hunting ends, and the work begins—and it's the huntin' that's fun. So ya kinda soft shoe it on up there for an hour or two, stop at a spring-fed stream—ice-cold—and drink your fill. Then keep on going till the sun's up about 10:00 high. Find a restin' ridge, look out across the valley, and breathe in all that mountain air. That's livin'.

HB and his son Ben bring home an 8-pointer. Virginia, 1973.

The mornings now in Brush Country are different. Sunup comes later now—cooler at 6:30 a.m. and still dark outside. Ya kinda begin to get the urge to break out the musket, look her over, load up a few rounds of ammo, and check to see if the sights still line up. 'Cause it ain't gonna be long before the real naggin' feeling comes to head for the high country. Get up there in them hills and get after them varmints. Listen to the crows call; watch the blue jays watch the chipmunks. Walk—just you and your musket. I love it. There ain't nothin' like it.

Come in to that ol' camp house after dark, cook up a big batch of creamed beef on toast, and hit the hay early, 'cause at 4:00 a.m., you're gonna be up again for another full day in the high country, slippin' through the woods, exploring, and matching wits with nature. It's fantastic. Well, if ya haven't been to the high country in the fall, ya best never go, 'cause it's easy to get the fever about this time of year. Ya kinda want to start planning to move out and get up high when the frost settles in on the rim rock. That feeling is already settling in, and I'm itching now to go up high as soon as the days get a little shorter and the nights a little cooler.

Being Poor Is a Relative Thing

I don't know if you've ever thought about this or not, but being poor—or as they say now, "under-privileged"—is a relative thing. And look at it from this perspective—danged if we (my family) weren't worse off in Depression days than are most folks who are now on welfare. The only thing was that we didn't know we were poor. As a matter of fact, we thought we were pretty well off—and we were, when compared to others. But by today's standards, we were desperate.

Well, we didn't have a refrigerator; we had an icebox. Neither did we have electric lights, because there wasn't any electricity. No electricity—HUD would be on that situation today: "Get those poor folks some electricity!" And what about the plumbing? Just one cold water faucet in the kitchen and two in the bathroom—that was all. No hot water heater! No commode! We had to beat a path to the outhouse behind the garage. Today, EPA wouldn't let you build an outhouse—even if you wanted one. Well, the outhouse was bad enough, but consider taking a bath at night in the wintertime.

First, you'd have to stoke up the fire in the kitchen stove and then put on a kettle of water to heat, and when it was hot, you'd run to the bathroom (only one), pour that water in the tub (and the tub was so cold that it would drop the temperature of your hot water) and then turn on the cold water—and you'd need just a little, or the water would be too cold. If that happened, you'd have to heat some more water. But anyway, you didn't need much water, because there was no heat in the bathroom. So you'd not be lounging around in that tub if the temperature was down around forty or so. But you needed some light, so you carried one of the two coal oil lamps. The folks would be using the other one in the kitchen. Before getting in the tub, set the lamp on the usual spot there in the bathroom. (In a few months, there'd be this big black ring on the ceiling overhead. Ya had that all over the house. Wherever ya set that lamp, the soot would collect in a circle on the ceiling.)

Anyway, get through with that bath, wrap a towel around ya, and dash for the one wood heater in Mom and Dad's bedroom. The family stayed there until bedtime, which wasn't long after dark. Git those pajamas on, take one last warm-up, and dash for the front bedroom. If it was thirty degrees outside, the chill factor wasn't quite so bad on the inside.

There was no telephone, no central air conditioning or heat—not even a fan. We had no mixer, no hot water, no inside plumbing (save a coupla cold water faucets), no vacuum cleaner, no electric lights, no refrigerator, and no TV. But ya know something? Those were some of the happiest years of my life, and I know many other folks who went through the same thing would also make that statement. Now I don't want to mislead anyone; we lived in a house that had been built only a year or so before the stock market crash. And we always had plenty of good food—many didn't have that. But our grocery bill probably never exceeded $5 a month. We ate what we grew, and we grew nearly everything. We only needed a little sugar, flour, salt, coffee, pepper, soda, and maybe baking powder, and that was about it. There weren't any paper towels, and Sears provided the TP, but everything else came from the farm—dairy products, butter and cream, lard, eggs, chicken, pork, and even our corn meal was ground from our corn right here in Devine.

The time from supper to bedtime was pleasant—particularly so after we had a radio. Sit there around that ol' stove listening to ol' Henry Aldridge or Fibber McGee and Molly, and everybody would be doing something—sewing, patching, or picking out peanuts or pecans. It was quiet. Today, we've lost that: TV blaring the latest insult to intelligence, dishwasher, washer and dryer going, someone talking on the telephone, someone else running the vacuum cleaner, and still another using the garbage disposal and electric mixer. The TV is making a weird sound from the mixer and vacuum, and you can't see the picture, which is no loss. But what I'm really saying is that by today's standards, we lived in poverty back there in the '30's—but that doesn't mean that the quality of life was any worse. In my view, the quality of life was better then. Nationwide, there was more pride and industry on the part of all people. If someone was down and out, you'd best be careful about offering to help, 'cause most didn't accept charity, even if offered in a friendly way. Pride would say, "We'll make it; we don't need no help." Contrast that with today when folks don't only ask for help (even if they don't need it); they demand it.

And the programs never seem to end. What so many of these programs do is take away initiative, destroy incentive, and absolutely demolish self-esteem. And what that does is eliminate any chance for a quality life. My advice to anyone of any race, creed, sex, or whatever is this: avoid participating in these government welfare programs. Don't do it. It isn't in your best interest long-term. It isn't in the nation's best interest. They basically serve the special interest groups, the bureaucrats, and some politicians. Being poor with pride isn't that bad. And if you have pride, you will not be poor but for a short time.

Hunting with Mark Crouch

A while back, I was out dove hunting with a buddy, which isn't too strange this time of year. But what was unusual was that this buddy was born when I was forty-six. There's some age spread there—but no matter if ya both like to hunt. My hunting partner was none other than Mark Crouch, age seven. Mark's brother, Kevin, was along too, but he's a little older and was out on his own. Earlier in the afternoon, Mark said he'd been on his own with a .410, and the doves were coming in pretty good. He'd kinda burned up his allotted number of shells and brought down two birds, which isn't too bad for a seven-year-old using a .410. Well, I had my limit and still had a few shells left, and Mark wanted to continue hunting. So we kicked around the question of a seven-year-old fella being large enough to shoot a sixteen-gauge shotgun. Mark said, "I kin do it. Let's go." I was more hesitant, but I said, "Okay, Mark; we'll give it a try. But we're gonna hunt like I hunted when I was a kid. In other words, we were gonna really *hunt* and not sit and wait for them to fly in to us." He was game, so off we went.

I put one shell in the automatic 16, and with safety on, we headed for some ol' mesquites up north of the tank. Sittin' out there a ways were three ol' doves kinda close together, and I said, "Now, Mark, we're gonna slip up on those doves, so you get in behind that mesquite, keep low, and don't make any noise." So we kinda snuck along there, and before long, Mark was in position to shoot.

"Mark," I whispered, "just kinda bring your gun up slowly, take good aim, hold right in between all three of those birds, and let 'er go." From the time he brought the gun up—which is about five inches longer than he is tall—all of about half a second elapsed before the ol' 16 roared and two doves dropped. Mark handed me the gun and was gone in a flash through the brush to retrieve the birds. He came back with them, and we climbed in under a mesquite. Loadin' in another shell, I said, "Mark, sit down here on my knee, and be real still. Next time, take a little longer when you aim."

"Okay," he said, alive, enthused, and ready. An ol' dove would come by and by, and he'd say, "Let me get that one."

"Uh, hold on, Mark; we'll wait until some of them wingers light over there in the same spot."

"Naw, let me get that one right there!"

"Too close, Mark; wouldn't be anything left but the feathers. Leave him alone, and we'll use him as a decoy and others will come sit. Look yonder, Mark—same tree, two birds there; take your time!"

Wham! Mark went tail end over teakettle as the ol' sixteen-gauge recoiled. Luckily, I caught the gun. He didn't even know he had landed on his back—he didn't have time to worry about it. He was gone after two more birds. Now he had six. Well, before too long, the sun was sinking, and ol' Mark had nine birds, which ain't bad for a seven-year-old hunting buddy. Mark said, "Uh, I like that sixteen." And I believe he did, but I don't know who had the better time—Mark or me. It's a great to see that kind of enthusiasm.

But anyway, I don't expect that Mark will shoot his birds from under a tree much longer. He'll soon be dropping them regularly out of the sky any day now. And I expect he'll always be interested in guns and hunting—real interested. Now hunting and guns are part of our national heritage. No matter how you look at it, it's true. Had it not been for guns and hunting, there would be no America. The pilgrims wouldn't have made it, Lewis and Clark wouldn't have accomplished what they did, and ol' Daniel Boone would have never been able to push westward towards Kentucky and Missouri. Even up to fairly recent times, hunting has provided an important part of the rural family's food supply.

So what's changed? Why do we now need to abandon hunting and private gun ownership? I want private ownership of guns continued and hunting continued, and if a person doesn't want to own a gun and doesn't want to hunt—fine. Don't buy a gun, and don't think about using one. But don't lean on those of us who do have these interests. I hope that one of these days, Mark will have the opportunity to sit with a seven-year-old boy and observe the enthusiasm and excitement which hunting provides. Now you can help assure that we can continue having the right to private ownership of guns and the right to hunt. The National Rifle Association has carried the ball for those of us who enjoy these rights. But the NRA is fed up with playing defense and is now going on the offense. They are attempting to eliminate some of the restraints that our bureaucratic friends and anti-hunting groups have imposed on us. You can become part of that effort by joining the NRA. Included in membership is the choice of two quality hunting magazines, gun theft insurance, and liability insurance while hunting. Joining the NRA will help to insure that Mark Crouch, his contemporaries, and those who follow will have the rights of gun ownership. Let's preserve these rights for those to come.

November 8, 1979

Bustles, Corsets, Jeans, and Greasy Hair

The other day, I was kinda looking through some old family photo albums, and I became interested in what folks wore way back in the good ol' days. Now there was this one photo of my grandfather with his brothers, sister, mother, and the in-laws. They were posing in front of my grandfather's home—about 1900 or so. Anyway, they were all dolled up—fit to kill, whatever that means. But the one thing that first got my attention was ol' Grandmom standing there, and I believe her waist must have been about twenty inches. Now I certainly don't believe Grandmom had a twenty-inch waist, 'cause she was a sizeable woman. But I reckon I know what caused that appearance. I don't profess to be an expert in these matters, but I've heard my parents discuss this subject. Anyway, Grandmom was probably wearing a corset configured with whalebone stays, and it probably took her and all of her sisters and sister-in-law to cinch that thing down to twenty inches. Well, then, she probably also had a bustle on, and what that thing did, they tell me, was to kinda make the skirt flare out in back. Ya wonder if all of that stuff came unwound all of a sudden—it'd be dangerous to be standing nearby.

I certainly couldn't have worn all that stuff. You'd have to make a concerted effort just to breathe, and all of that constriction would give me a headache. Anyway, that's the first thing that caught my eye—and the next thing was that ol' Granpop had on this dark suit, as did the others. Apparently, there wasn't a dry cleaner in those days, 'cause in every picture I've ever seen of those times, it appears that the men needed to have their pants pressed. They only fastened the top button on their coats, and that fad was in fashion for a long time. So that's a wee bit about how they dressed in the olden days.

First generation of Briscoes in Devine, circa 1900.
L-R: George T. Briscoe Sr., Susie Robinson Briscoe, JF (Tobe) Briscoe,
Mollie Robinson Briscoe, John A. Whitfield, Lena Briscoe Whitfield,
Notley Briscoe, Mary Briscoe. Seated: Mary Gray Briscoe.

Now as to my father's generation—those folks kinda put on the dog. In an old family album, there are many photos that were taken on picnics, hunting trips, camping—all on Sunday afternoon when TV and the NFL were unheard of. Well, what does a body do if there's no TV? Well, you put on your best duds—meaning dark suit and top hat—harness up the team and hitch it to the hack, buggy, or whatever, go jump a bunch of gals, and head on down to the closest railway bridge. The gals will all have on long white dresses and big hats, and ya kinda hang around the bridge there and cut up a little. I, too, prefer a little class in my apparel choices, but top hats, suits, and white dresses on a railway bridge picnic are a bit much. However, I have this ol' book of photos taken all over America in the early 1900s, and apparently everybody dressed for picnics and tree-climbing like that—can't deny they had class.

The second generation of Briscoes in Devine circa 1910:
Standing: George T. Briscoe, Jr., Minnie Briscoe, John Briscoe,
Stell Briscoe, L.G. Briscoe. Seated: Kate Briscoe DuBose, George
T. Briscoe, Sr., Susie Robinson Briscoe, Brian Briscoe.

Then, further on, when I was a teenager, dudes routinely stood around with a pound or two of bear grease in their hair—greasy kid stuff. Look at a photo of ol' Clark Gable back there, and ya know he used at least a pint of Vaseline Hair Tonic to get all of that hair slicked back. Can't ya just see the gals running their hands through that? But the gals weren't too cool, either. They wore long skirts and bobby socks and screamed every time Frank Sinatra started to sing. When the bobby socks went outta style, there came this crazy contraption called a chemise. Any gal who wore one of those things automatically took on the shape of an avocado. Now, for those shaped like an avocado, it was fine. But it put the rest to a distinct disadvantage, curve-wise. Fortunately, the chemise soon lost its appeal.

Coming down to the sixties in my kids' generation, things really went downhill. The teenage girls began to iron their hair and let it grow as long as possible. I had one daughter who had a great many concentrated orange juice cans, and at night, she would wash her hair, dry it, and then iron it. Finally, she'd roll it up on those cans and go to bed. She looked like a walking garbage heap, and how in the world she slept is beyond me. Then the fashion world was hit with the mini-skirt. My wife and I are somewhat conservative, and we said, "No short-short skirts." So when this older daughter left for school in the mornings, she'd start rollin' up the skirt to mid-thigh or higher. But when she came home, she'd forget to roll it back down, and the discussions would begin.

Then came a fad that hasn't gone out yet—blue jeans. To really be cool, a person had to have the dirtiest, scrounge-iest, oiliest, hole-iest, smelliest jeans around. The pant legs needed to be too long so you'd walk on them. I've seen my daughters spend three hours on their hair, two hours on their faces, and then put on a pair of scroungy jeans. Well, the long jeans were bad enough. but along came the cut-offs. They were still scroungy for both boys and girls—really gross.

But the one person who saved the fashion scene for America was Farrah Fawcett. Ol' Farrah Hydrant—or whatever—was (and still is) a girl with better-than-average looks. To some, she'd be downright appealing. Anyway, ol' Farrah came out with this hairdo which could only be duplicated if'n ya had a blowdryer. Personally, I believe that Farrah was—and is—part of a conspiracy on the part of those who manufacture the durned dryers. No dryer manufactured in the US will continue operating after ten hours of use—that's three hair-dryings. They are designed and manufactured to self-destruct after ten hours. If ol' Farrah hadn't come along and brought us the blow dryer, I could have had two new pickups. But I really don't need two new pickups, and it was worth it to see the ironed hair and scroungy jeans fad phased out. Thank you, Farrah.

Well, all of that is crazy, but that's the way it was—and is. But we've not seen the end—or the bottom—because now we are going lower than ever. Today, if you aren't a walking bumper sticker, you ain't cool. Ya gotta have all these signs on ya. Some are downright obscene, and folks walk around in public proclaiming by T-shirt that they are the world's greatest something or other. That's the pits.

But no matter—if ya don't like the current fad, stick around a while; it'll change. And it might be better, a la Farrah. But one thing for certain—corsets, bustles, bobbysocks, greasy kid stuff, miniskirts, chemises, whatever—if some clown designs it and it becomes fashionable, folks will wear it. *No le hace.*

Think *Sausage* Before You Shoot

Back yonder, when I was a young buck, I didn't use much discretion when it came to hunting. If the season was on and fair game came in range, that was it—the decision was automatic. As I've grown older, though, I've become a little more cautious, and everything must be okay before I shoot. Take last year, for example—I was out there, sittin' up in this ol' oak tree using just a plain ol' 30-30 with open sights. Whatever shot I'd take couldn't be very long, 'cause I could see for only a short distance in either direction along this right-of-way. Anyway, near sunset, a chill done flat settled in there in that live oak flat. It was real cold. But when the sun was almost touching the horizon, I could hear a critter moving my way through the heavy layer of leaves that blanketed the ground. So I got that ol' Winchester to the ready position and waited while the chill and excitement brought on shivers and shakes. In a short time, I could see the grey form through the live oak branches, and shortly, under the very next oak over was a buck coming my way. It was a fork horn—fat-looking dude. At that point, all of these considerations came into mind—nice deer, season almost over, directly under my tree, can drive the truck right up to him—those were the pluses. Then on the other side of the coin—sun setting, cold as the dickens, only a fork horn, a lot of work after the shot is fired, and so on. The result was that that ol' buck is still out there some place, and he never knew that for a moment he stood not more than fifteen feet from some who a few years back might have tacked his horns up in the garage. Anyway, youngsters are apt to shoot and think later, and that brings me to a recent Thanksgiving morning.

Ol' Ben, my son, was out early, and not long after he settled in the blind, a six-pointer came along, and he didn't consider many factors except that he was deer hunting, and here was a pretty fair buck. That was the end of consideration—*bang* went the .270, and the work began. My family celebrated the Thanksgiving holidays by putting that deer up. I recon everyone goes about that task in a different way, but we kinda make it a family project, and as most of you know, it's no easy task. Here's how we go about it: we skin and clean the deer as soon as possible. Then, if it's cold enough, we hang the carcass in the garage to cure for a coupla days. If it isn't cold enough, then we quarter the carcass and put it in an ol' refrigerator we have for that purpose. When cutting-up time comes, we take the back strap or tenderloin and cut that in very thin, round slices that fit well in a biscuit. But all of the rest of the deer goes into sausage, 'cause the Briscoes really love deer sausage.

By the time you take away all the fat, gristle, and other undesirable parts, you'll have about twenty-five pounds of venison. Then you've got to have about an equal amount of pork fat to venison for sausage. We make it the old-timey way—by hand. We use an old green grinder contraption to grind the venison and pork fat together. Once you've got a small mountain of meat, the seasoning starts. Personally, I like my sausage spicy, so I throw all of those weeds and seeds and herbs and peppers and garlic in there until everyone starts sneezing and their eyes start watering and the sausage gets kinda dry. Then you fry up a few test patties to check your flavor. After a few test-and-re-season exercises, you'll be ready to stuff those hog casins with an ol' hand-operated stuffer. Tie those "green" sausages off with string, tie the ends together to make a fat sausage loop, and you're ready for the smoking.

So right now, it's a clear, beautiful Sunday afternoon. The family worked almost all day Saturday on that deer, and now the smoking is underway. I use an ol' homemade smoker that was made from an angle iron frame that our milk cans use to sit in years ago. It's lightweight and easy to move around, so ya can face it into the wind. But anyway, get that fire started first; then get all the sausage links placed on the rods, and put the cover on. When the coals are ready, take a shovel, and put them in the covered hole just in front of the sausages. I put some green hickory branches in the coals for a great hickory-smoked flavor. Every now and then, ya can even add some live oak leaves and also a few hickory nuts. The nuts are good, because they make smoke for a longer period. Well, by the time ya smoke it, wrap it in foil, put it in a plastic bag, and put it into the deep freeze, it'd be worth about $9.00 a pound if your time is worth anything. But ya can't buy sausage like that, and some would say no one would want to—but we like it, and it ain't a bad way to spend the Thanksgiving holidays. Well, considering all of that work, you can bet I'm not about to bring down just any buck until the kids get back home for Christmas.

Christmas 1978. L-R: Ben Briscoe, Kate Briscoe Eastburn, Marianne Briscoe Outlaw, HB, Sue Briscoe Lindstrom Stewart, Roger Lindstrom, Mary Briscoe.

Horns Hooked

Like many of you, I've always been a big football fan. And I hope I never lose interest in the game. I'm really not that much interested in pro ball. About the only pro games I watch with any regularity are the Monday night games. But I'm really interested in high school and college ball. When it comes to college, it's the Southwest Conference. Since we have children in three Southwest conference schools, it might seem difficult to determine which school has priority in our support, but it really isn't that difficult. My wife and I are both Texas Techsans, and so is one daughter. Two daughters line up with Baylor, and our one son is an Aggie. But when it comes down to who I would rather have win, it's *always* the Texas Tech Red Raiders. But after that, I reckon, comes Baylor and A&M with equal priority. Then I'd have to lump SMU, TCU, and Rice in one category with one not having priority over the other. Down near the bottom is Texas and Houston in a dead heat. At the very bottom is Arkansas. If Moscow and Havana had teams in the SWC, it would almost be a tossup as to who I'd prefer to win—Arkansas, Moscow, or Havana.

Anyway, last weekend, we were up there at the annual Texas/A&M bash. We arrived there in time for the bonfire on Friday evening. There must have been some ten to fifteen thousand folks—mostly Aggies—around there. They were kinda working up a hate against the Sips—T-sippers, Horns, or whatever you want to call those dudes. Anyway, the Aggies ain't got much to do, so they spent most of the fall cutting logs and stacking them up on end, tied together with baling wire. They had quite a stack there. It must have been fifty feet or so at the base—maybe more. And it was probably fifty or sixty feet high. At the top was this outhouse, and some of the Aggies said that if it fell before midnight, the Aggies would win—otherwise the Horns might. Anyway, along about 8:00 p.m., the Aggie band cranked up, and these yell leaders (Mark Outlaw from the Devine suburb of Moore is one) had some torches, and with appropriate ruffles and flourishes and some kind of weird maneuvers, they finally lit the fire. Now, for Aggies, the bonfire stack was pretty well engineered. It's my feeling that they hired an engineer from Tech to do the work for them. But they'd run this three-quarter-inch pipe up the middle of the stack of logs and pumped some ol' contaminated JP-4—that's jet fuel to those who don't know. And they'd pump a great batch up there, which kinda ran down the sides and soaked that entire pile. Anyway, when they put the torches to that pile of logs, it exploded in flames, working up a hate campaign against the Horns in all those Aggies. There wasn't a Hook 'em Horns guy in the bunch. But there was a big bunch of Aggies behind us. They kept hollerin', "Beat the Hell out of Iran." I reckon they thought A&M was playing Iran the next day even though Iran doesn't have a team.

Well, the hate campaign finally ended after a few emotional speeches by Jacob Green, the defensive end (who is listed on the program at 230 and looks more like 270), Curtis Dickey, and a few other guys who kinda wanted to end their college careers by beatin' the Horns. When the bonfire ended, there was still a great flame goin', and after a good night's rest, it was still going the next morning. That Tech engineer did a good job.

On Saturday morning, we were up and had breakfast about 9:00, and the crowd started to arrive around 9:30, if you can believe that. The game didn't start until 1:30! But it is always like that at A&M. It was a crazy thing—by 10:00, you couldn't find a parking place anywhere. Even these guys with burnt orange on began to arrive early. I can understand the Aggies doing something like that, but the T-sips? Well, then folks parked their cars and commenced to open up their trunks, unloading lawn chairs and a card table, and before long, they'd be eating, right there in the parking lot. Not just a few were doing that; they all were. We'd spent the night in a motor home about a block south of the stadium, and it was interesting to watch all those goings on. Then about 10:30, the Aggie band cranked up again, and all of the corps guys (and gals) formed up, and they started marching over towards the stadium. You know, the Aggies are kinda slow. It's nearly two blocks from the Corps area to Kyle Field, so three hours early will put them there about on time.

Bonfire for the UT-A&M game, 1979.

But sometime around 11:00-ish, the band and the Corps arrived, and you could hear them down there under the stands, going through their yells. By 11:00, the stadium was half-full. Crazy. They didn't want to miss anything. Pretty soon, the Corps starts marching in. It was still two hours from game time, and it's already a good show.

Well, before you know it, there's 69,000 other folks in that stadium. That's about three times as many people as there are in Medina County, and they paid $8.50 each to see the game. That's a pretty good sum of cash. But anyway, you talk about pageantry, excitement, thrill, and a lot of hoopla—they had it. I kinda think the T-Sips were of the mind that they'd go on down to College Station, get that game over with, and get on to the Sugar Bowl. The Aggs were of a different mind, so they hung tough. At halftime, they were ahead 13–7. They were also ahead 13–7 at game's end. Over there, across the field, some thirty thousand or so college kids were carryin' on, and whenever the band played this bit about "saw varsity's horns off," all them Aggies were singing, and they kinda had their arms around each other, leaning in one direction and then the other, like they were sawing. It was wild—crazy.

Anyway, when the game was over, we jumped down on the playing field and went across to see what the Longhorn band was up to. They were sitting there like statues. We thought they were going to play a concert or something. The truth was, they weren't going to play anything. They couldn't, because they were in shock. The Aggies had won. The Horns—they'll be going to the Sun Bowl. For the Aggies, they'd just won their Bowl game, and all the ol' Aggie exes grinned and shouted, "Gig 'em." They folded up their motorhomes and loudly stole away with their auto horns tooting "Goodbye to Texas University; so long to the orange and the white."

It was a nice weekend for the Aggs.

Dropping Bulldozers in the Arctic

I don't know if many of you have spent any time in Alaska or not, but that's great country. However, you've got to be some kind of a nut to want to live up there. In my earlier years, I often thought I'd like to spend a three-year tour there, and in some ways I'm kinda sorry it never came to be. But even though I didn't spend three years there, I did spend a considerable amount of time in Alaska, and one time I was there for a period of six weeks. It was in 1956 during the International Geophysical Year. My takeaway from those six weeks is: "there ain't no way to get used to Alaska."

During that six-week time period, we were flying supplies out to an Ice Island for the scientific folks who were to set up camp for the summer. The summer pretty much consists of July 4. The rest is winter, and there on the island, it might get up to 36 degrees in midsummer. But I don't believe I would have made it even for those six weeks if I hadn't been young and in pretty good physical condition. We'd load up that ol' C-124 Globemaster—a four-engine prop-driven underpowered machine—with some thirty thousand pounds or so and head north about six hours out over the polar ice cap from Fairbanks. It was a wild mission. On one of our first missions, my crew and I dropped a bulldozer that was to be used to clear a runway. I'll never forget that. There was no timing line or anything to use for aiming our drop; we just kinda came over the drop zone at 2,500 feet, started counting when the impact point was blotted out by the radar, and let her rip. Sixteen thousand pounds were suspended from four parachutes that were each sixty-four feet in diameter. One chute didn't open, and by the time I could rack that ol' bird up, the bulldozer had hit the ground—ice. We missed the impact point by only about thirty yards, and that was luck. In ten minutes, they had that thing running.

The next time around, though, we weren't so lucky. There were twenty-four barrels of fuel for the dozer, and they were all fastened together on a roller conveyor ramp. You had to have everything timed just right so that the loadmaster, scanner, and anyone else available could get the twelve thousand pounds moving down the conveyors. As we neared the drop zone again, we got the signal to cut that bunch of barrels loose so they'd start rolling down the conveyor. Well, they were cut loose, but they didn't start rolling fast enough. When we were at drop time, the barrels hadn't cleared the plane yet. I called, "No drop," and the scanner called back and said, "No way; them barrels is moving, and there's no way we can stop them—they're gone." We missed the ice island with twenty-four barrels, but we didn't miss it too far, and the ground crew was able to recover them with a weasel snow machine.

Well, in a couple days or so, the dozer driver had a runway built on that ice island that was about five thousand feet long. So then we could come in there and land on the ice. If you thought about it too much as a pilot, it could make you kinda queasy to come in there with a 165,000-pound aluminum cloud and set her down on ice right smack in the middle of the Arctic Ocean. And the worse thing was that this ice island wasn't a true ice island. A true ice island is a chunk that has broken off the continental shelf and can be up to 150 feet thick. This island was really just a large chunk of regular Arctic Ocean ice, and at the thickest, it was about twelve feet and at the thinnest, about eight feet. Anyhow, they had a little beacon out there, and of course, we had to have the beacon, or we could never find the place. We drew up an instrument approach to the runway using the beacon.

One time we made an approach when fog and ice crystals covered everything and visibility registered at zero. I flew in on our instrument approach, and the idea was to drop right down to about one hundred feet on final approach, trusting that when ya broke out of the overcast, you'd be lined up with the runway so's ya could land. We had everything hacked right on down there, but when we finally were down to where we could see a little bit, the darned runway was all out of alignment. The island had turned and shifted around, and the runway had then assumed a different heading. I flew around for a few minutes, decided it was hopeless, and then climbed back to cruise altitude and went back home. Thirteen hours after takeoff, we were back at Fairbanks, and the day was all for naught.

I'll never forget another trip in to that crazy ice island. We landed there on the ice and unloaded. The engineer and scanner were inspecting the plane, and the engineer reached in and just picked up a great chunk of the exhaust collector ring and some of the exhaust stacks and dropped them down on the ice. Well, what do you do with something like that? There wasn't much choice. You either abandon the airplane there on the ice or fly her out. That's what we did—cranked all four engines up for takeoff, and then as soon as we were airborne, shut the bad engine down and came on back to Fairbanks on three engines. We spent seven hours on three engines, and we had to climb slowly up to ten thousand to clear the Brooks Range on the way back. We made it on only three engines, but we could have started the damaged engine up in the air in case of an emergency.

Well, all of this was happening in May and June, so it was never dark for the entire six weeks. We'd be up flying and preparing for our next mission for fifteen hours or so. Then we'd get back in to Fairbanks, and they'd have a softball game going in broad daylight at 3:00 in the morning. We'd get in on that and then go have a bull session, and before long, it'd be 8:00 in the morning, which is no time to go to bed.

It was a crazy pace and a crazy place.

Hog-Killin' Time

When I was a kid, one of the busier times of the year arrived with the winter season when the first real cold front came in. And that was hog-killin' time. Personally, I always looked forward to that time, but I kinda doubt my parents were that crazy about it, 'cause hog-killin' was work—a lot of work.

We'd begin around 9:00 in the mornin' after the milking was done. Dad would have this porker fed out, and he'd take the ol' .22 out there to the hog pen, and ya know—right there between the eyes. That'd be it for the ol' porker. Then ya gotta get in there and stick that ol' hog so's he'd bleed properly. After that was done, he'd be drug over by the wash house where the fire was going under the wash pot. The water in the pot would be boilin' hot, and next to the wash house was a cable to heave that ol' hog up. Dad would get a bucketful of hot water and begin to pour it on him. He'd continue pouring until the hair slipped, and then everyone would start scraping—that is, ya had to scrape the hair off. The boiling water was used to get him where he'd scrape clean. There are hog-scraping tools—mostly used up north—but Dad just preferred a butcher knife.

The scraping was no easy chore, but eventually, we'd have all the hair off, and then Dad would make a cut at the Achilles tendon at the rear feet and insert the single tree hooks so's ya could attach the block and tackle and just raise him up head-down. Once ya got him hefted up there, you'd be ready for the—well, guttin'. I never cared much for that part of it, but it had to be done. And gross as it may sound, we didn't throw much away. "Used everything but the squeal," they used to say. The head, of course, was used to make "hogshead cheese," which was a type of cheesy sauce, and there's nothin' that'll make a better sandwich. Now, one thing we didn't save was the feet, although some pickled 'em; we just did without.

When ya get through cleanin' that ol' hog, you'd pull him way up there on the windmill, and he'd hang there overnight. The next morning, the work would really begin. Ya don't skin a porker; now that'd really be work. So ya just cut him up. First remove the hams—and they'd be three made ready for the curing and smoking. Then, if I remember correctly, we always made sausage out of the shoulder, although some make ham out of them. We liked sausage better 'n ham. Then ya had to cut the side meat, which was the bacon. Pork ribs were made ready, too. Next ya took all of that fat and cut it in one-inch squares and put them in the wash pot. It'd have a fire around it, and the lard-making would be underway. Before long, fat would be rendered out, and all that would be left would be the small, brown, crisp cracklins.

Well, those cracklins weren't that bad; now they're sold for appetizers, but those ain't real cracklins. Mom'd strain those cracklins and put them in a bucket there on the back porch. Then every now and then, she'd make cornbread for the dogs, and it would be full of cracklins. The dogs really loved cracklin' bread. Once in a while, when I was feeding the dogs, I had to try a little of that stuff—and ya know what, from that time on, I ate with the dogs.

You'd also have to make some soap, so you'd save some of the fat squares. After you'd get it heatin' a bit, you'd put the lye in there and get to stirrin' and mixin' the brew. When everything looked about right, quit the cookin' and let the soap set up. Mom would take a butcher knife and cut the soap in squares and put them in a box on the back porch. We didn't have detergents in those days; we had lye soap, which was powerful strong.

Then came the pork sausage. Hand-grind the pork, then several rounds of season-cook-taste. When it was ready to stuff, mom brought over the casings: small intestines.

Finally, put all of the sausage, ham, and bacon there in the smokehouse, and start that ol' fire going. When it was all done—I used to love to walk into that smoke house and smell that food—out of this world! But I think most of all, I used to enjoy breakfast the morning after the hog-killing 'cause we'd have backstrap. That's the tenderloin. Mom would slice it real thin, fry it, and put it in a buttered biscuit and I'd have that with a cup of coffee—no way you could spit that out. I mean, that was downright good—love it.

Finally, when ya got everything put away, you'd start deliverin' some of the choice bits around to the neighbors. Then, when they killed a hog, you'd get some of their fresh meat. That's the way it was back there in the good ol' days at hog-killin' time.

BRUSH COUNTRY BULL 1980

Discipline

Back there in the good ol' days, you could count the number of law enforcement officers in the Medina County on the fingers of one hand. There was a county sheriff, and maybe he had a deputy. Then one game warden probably covered two or three counties. Devine had a night watchman. Hondo had one, too, and that was about it.

Well, it's true that the county population was much smaller in those days. I can well remember that the number of folks in Devine was about nine hundred or so there in the thirties. But relatively speaking, today we are loaded when it comes to the number of law enforcement people. Counting constables, city policemen, game wardens, county sheriffs and deputies, department of Public Safety (Highway Patrol) officers, and on and on, there are probably close to fifty law enforcement people in Medina County.

"Well, good grief, you folks musta lived in absolute terror back in the good ol' days with so few law enforcement folks." Naw, that ain't true. We lived in peace back in them days. We live in *terror* now. "Well, if'n that's so, whose fault is it?" It certainly isn't the law enforcement folks' fault! Really, we need more law enforcement people now. They can't keep up with the present workload. The real answer is that it is the fault of our society. So let's kinda take a look at this situation.

In all of the time I lived with my folks as a youngster, I can never remember locking our house. There weren't even locks on the doors. When we went to bed at night, windows and doors were unlocked and open; just the screen doors and windows kept the insects out. Many of you who are younger can remember when it was possible to park a truck downtown with tools, guns, and whatever in it, unlocked, and leave it there all day. When you came back, it'd all be there. Try that today. You can have nothing in your truck, lock it, and chain the steering wheel, and when you come back thirty minutes later, you'll be lucky if the truck is there. In the good ol' days, there was no drug problem. There was discipline in the schools and at home. My folks said, "You get a whipping at school; you'll get another when you get home." Now most folks say, "You get a whipping at school; we'll whup the principal." (Or get a lawyer and sue him and the school.)

The fourth generation of Briscoes and friends in Devine, 1971, brought up under discipline and rules, "most of which make sense."
L-R: Ben Briscoe, Jimmy Briscoe, Terry McAnelly, Sue Briscoe, Rusty McAnelly, Crouch girls, Henry Briscoe, Marianne Briscoe, GH Briscoe, Kate Briscoe, Mary Ann McAnelly, Charlie Crouch and daughter, Inie Briscoe, Carol Crouch, Ray Briscoe, Nancy Briscoe McAnelly.

Back in the good ol' days, if a teacher or principal or anyone with the school found you downtown after school, they'd say, "Get home. You have no business down here." Well, that wasn't all. In the good ol' days, the crime rate was almost zero. Now, a coupla years back, a President's Commission on Crime spent $2 million studying what to do about crime and how to lower the rate. Know what they decided to do about the crime rate? Simple—all ya do is not categorize certain offenses as criminal, like possession of pot and pot-smoking, theft under certain dollar values, etc. If you don't call that crime, then the crime rate will naturally go down—beautiful! They must have had some marvelous minds on that commission.

Well, it's our society that is to blame for all of this. And we pay for it. Approximately fifty law enforcement folks now work in this county. That costs us money. Most of those folks have to have a car with a radio to patrol in. That costs us money. And then we kinda need more courts and judges. That costs us money, too. And don't think that it doesn't cost us money just to feed the losers over in the crossbar hotel. And if they want a lawyer, you and I will provide one at the rate of $50 an hour. Bad as those things are, they are not the only way we pay. And they aren't the worst. The worst is being held at gunpoint and robbed, as one Devine citizen was recently. The worst is coming home to your castle—your sanctuary—and finding it ransacked. The worst is the cost of installing burglar alarms, foolproof locks, and on and on. The absolute worst is getting killed by a DWI.

Our society made a wrong turn back there when Earl Warren was appointed as Chief Justice of the Supreme Court. Our society made a wrong turn when Benjamin Spock decided to write a book on how to raise babies. Our society made a wrong turn when organizations such as the American Civil Liberties Union began to take up cases of the ten-time losers who prey on you and me.

Okay, so what do we do about it? First, if you used one of Dr. Spock's books on how to raise children, throw it away and start all over. A child needs to be brought up under discipline. You can't have a wholesome society if everybody does his own thing. That child may as well learn early on that ours is a complex society and that he must lie under certain rules, most of which make sense. Then, in case the child doesn't get that upbringing at home—and many will not—there should be discipline in the schools. I mean that young people should behave themselves properly when in school and the administration should see that they do. When confronted with a ten-time loser who can only disrupt class, cause trouble, and be an all-around bad guy, boot him.

The fifth generation of Briscoes of Devine 2002—dedicated to "bringing 'em up right." L-R: Standing: Weston Stewart, Mark Outlaw, Marianne Outlaw, Kate Briscoe Eastburn, Daniel Eastburn, Mark Stewart, Sue Briscoe Lindstrom Stewart, Erin Stewart, Charli Eastburn Groen, Emalee Stewart Smith, Emily Mann Briscoe, Ben T. Briscoe. Seated: Colby Stewart, Taylor Eastburn, Ellee Stewart, Mary Briscoe, Henry Briscoe, Jarod Briscoe. Children: Colton Briscoe, Tess Outlaw, Kayla Stewart, Addison Outlaw, Dillon Briscoe.

Now I don't mean to imply that a lack of discipline is in any way due to the school administration. I'm talking about all of America. And what you see in the schools is a reflection of, again, our society with its lax discipline at home, in the streets, and in the schools. Now personally, I am a disciplinarian. I suppose that's because of the way I was brought up and because of a twenty-five-year military career. I believe in self-discipline. There's no way we can hire enough law enforcement folks to assign one to each loser our society produces. So I say, let's produce fewer losers. Let's have courts that are fair, but bone tough. Let's make the penalty such that it is consistent with the crime. Let's shed the liberal permissive judges. Let's have a judicial system that doesn't take ten years or more to determine guilt or innocence.

Let's get back to basics. Insist and insist and insist that these things be done. And then you will pay fewer taxes. You'll need fewer burglar alarms and fewer law enforcement people. We may live longer, safer lives. Even better, those would-be losers might not be losers after all if brought up right. They would have an opportunity for a quality life. What happens in this regard depends on you and me and what we do.

Lucky Strike Goes to War

I reckon there's one thing about kids that's universal, and that is if something is cool, they've *got* to try it—whether it makes sense or not. Take back there when I was a kid. First big difference was that "cool" only happened when a blue norther blew in. That term "cool" was unheard of in those days except to describe the weather. But other than that, it was the okay thing in those days to smoke. Back then, few women smoked. Some of the old-timers did, but very few. It wasn't fashionable in those days until some of the movie queens began to smoke; then before long, almost everyone did. The surgeon general, I reckon, was concerned about other matters, and the fact that all of the lifetime smokers were dying in their forties and fifties was just because they died from old age. Anytime a person died and was thirty-five or so and the doc couldn't explain it, they just died of old age.

Anyway, smoking is one of the things I never got hooked on, and I reckon it was for three reasons: one was that for most of my young life, I was involved in athletics, and the coaches didn't want a person to smoke. The other thing was that my parents didn't think that smoking was such a good thing for a youngster, and the third thing was that, of course, I had to try smoking, and the quality of materials I smoked kinda convinced me that smoking was terrible. Here are some examples.

You're about ten years old—or maybe even eleven-plus—out there in the corn field on a Sunday afternoon with a couple of your buddies, and you've got a few kitchen matches … ya know. Just kinda take one of those ol' dried-out corn stalks and break ya a piece off. The ol' stalk will snap nicely at the joints, and you'll have a piece of smoking material about five inches long and the size of a cigar. The ol' stalk is porous, and you can draw on it real good. Just put that thing in your mouth, light it up, and get to puffing. There's only one way to describe it—terrible. It tastes just like burning corn stalks. Well, cancel out the cornstalk idea. So hop on down to the creek, and there's a bunch of Mustang grapevines. Now a piece of grapevine is made for smoking. It's hollow, and ya can draw on it real well, but it's a bugger to keep it lit. Once it's lit, you soon hope it'll go out, 'cause it tastes like burning wood—better than a cornstalk, but still terrible. Strike two.

Ya still haven't exhausted all of the resources, because there's cedar bark. Just get you a piece of ol' newspaper—any kind of paper will do—and peel you a little of that cedar bark. Kinda crush it all up and roll your own into a nice-looking fag. Well, light that thing up, and *whew*—get just one of them cedar cinders down your gullet, and you can check off the cedar bark cigar. It was worse than terrible. Well, I was down to my last best idea. The reason I came on to this idea is that I'd seen the hands do this many times, so I tried. My mom had some ol' fig trees there in the back yard, and of course, every now and then, the leaves would die and turn brown. Close by, you had these corn shucks. Just crush up some of those fig leaves real fine and roll them up in one of them corn shucks, and you'd have a real cigaroot. Now crushed fig leaves don't hang together that well, and the shuck ain't that good, either. Before long, you might have the whole mess in your mouth—fire and all. Somehow, I reckon those ideas I mentioned above are why I never developed the smoking habit. To me, regardless of how cool it was supposed to have looked, I couldn't stand the taste of burning cornstalk, cedar bark, newspaper, grapevine, shucks, and fig leaves.

In those days, too, smokeless tobacco—Skoal or whatever—wasn't a big thing, at least with youngsters. Sure, they had Brown Mule and Day's Work, but for some reason or other, that wasn't very appealing—mostly 'cause ya only had to bite off a chew of that Brown Mule one time and after being sicker than two horses or mules, you'd give that up, too.

A big thing back in those days for the older folks was Dukes Mixture and Bull Durham. Ya needed to have that round tag hanging out of your shirt pocket. That was just as in then as the round tin can in the back of your jeans is today. Take that ol' sack of Bull Durham out of your shirt pocket. It would have the papers in under the label that went around the sack. Get you a thin paper, and then ya kinda roll up the sides so's they'd be vertical. Then with your right hand, ya kinda poured and tapped with your index finger till you had the right amount of tobacco in there. Hold one end of the string between your right index finger and thumb and then get the other end in between your teeth and pull on it. That'd close the sack. Stick the sock back in your pocket and then finish rolling up the fag—and ya had to lick it to seal it. Put that thing in between your teeth or over in the side of your mouth and then take a kitchen match outta your khaki pants pocket. Start low down on your pants, and pull that ol' match on up your pants real fast, and the friction would light it. After ya got the cigarette going, there'd be a coupla tongue spits to get those little pieces of tobacco out of your mouth that was dangling from the cigarette.

Well, that's about the way it was for those who smoked in the olden days. It tasted terrible, and it was too much trouble. And I'm kinda glad it was. 'Cause to this day, I never got the habit, and at this late date, I don't plan on getting it, either. Besides that, as I've gotten older, it hasn't made much sense to pay good money for something that you set fire to and burnt up while it was in your mouth. Whew—that's crazy! And real crazy when you know it might give you lung cancer.

Well, if'n you have a youngster or two around the house, just leave some cornstalks, cedar bark, newspaper, grape vines, fig leaves, and kitchen matches around handy and see if he gets the idea. He might burn your house down, but he might just kick the smoking habit before it ever gets started.

Flying Fish and Onions

For the earlier part of my time in the Air Force, I flew the troop carriers—or as the troops called it, the trash carrier. Now that term wasn't directed at the folks we carried, but at the gear we hauled. Sometimes it was really weird. Take one morning—I was there in Japan, flying the ol' C-54 headed for Korea. Just before going to the airplane, I checked in the area of the terminal, and they said, "Haven't much weight on that machine, but it is spaced out." Every available inch of space in the cargo compartment was used. So I was kinda interested to know if we had a load of feathers or whatever. So I get on out there to the plane, and it was loaded with Kotex. For the troops in Korea? Well, for those who don't know, Kotex was used as a filter in the cooling system of a F-51 (P-51 for you WWII types)—weird.

Then on another trip to Korea, I checked with the terminal guys, and they said, "You're gonna love this load." So at the plane, I checked in with the loadmaster, and he said, "Uh, we got ten thousand pounds of onion plants—whew!" We didn't have to make many position reports that morning. As we passed over the ground stations, they'd smell us: "Uh, you them guys with the load of onions?"

Well, sometimes those ol' planes would break down, and you could be delayed at a bad time. Take the time I was headed out of Hawaii down to Johnston Island and then on to Kwajalein and Eniwetok. That was plenty of times, but this morning, I got out to the plane, and she was loaded with some chow for the folks who were working down range in the anti-ballistic missile program. Now most of those folks were from Hawaii, and that means most were of oriental extraction. And folks of oriental extraction—at least those in Hawaii—like fish, and that's what the plane was loaded with—25,000 pounds of frozen fish. Big ol' fish were frozen solid, and they were kinda stacked in there like cordwood and secured to pallets with nets. Well, everything went A-okay until we started the takeoff roll, and for some reason or other, we had to abort the takeoff and return to the flightline for maintenance. About four hot hours later, we were ready to go again. But same thing—another abort. It weren't too many more hot hours on that flight line till them fish began to thaw out. Them thawed fish were slick and slimy and totally unmanageable. They were siding all over the place. Ya just couldn't secure those scaly rascals. Finally we had to cancel out and turn that mess over to the terminal folks.

HB in the cockpit of a C-124, 1953.

Then sometimes what ya hauled could have a pretty high priority. Back there in 1958, the US was hurryin' with the space program—trying to catch up to the Russians. In that and later years, I made many a trip in to Cape Canaveral hauling missiles and components. But this one Sunday afternoon, I was there in sunny California loading our cargo when this two-star general shows up.

He had some strong words for me. In so many words, he said, "Hey, Dad, you are hauling the second stage of our only Vanguard missile, and the President of the United States has a personal interest in this mission. I want you to know that if you land at a sink rate of more than three hundred feet per minute, the missile will collapse—and so will your career, so do your best." He didn't need to add that last remark. We made it all right, but when we finally arrived at the Cape, they said, "Uh, now you need to take that up to Baltimore. They are gonna match the first and second stages up there." There was more sweating, but we made it all right.

Well, we hauled just about anything almost everywhere, and although it became kinda tiresome flying all over the world, it wasn't boring.

Can You Afford This House?

I'm not much on book reports, but today I'm going to report on one that I think every American should read. The name of this book is *Can You Afford This House* and it has nothing to do with real estate. It refers to the House of Representatives in the United States Congress. Who was it written by? Well, by members of the House who are so concerned about what is happening there that they feel compelled to do something. Contributing to this book was one way to keep the people informed

Too much of today's legislation is bad. Have you ever wondered why? This might provide an answer. The House members vote for or against bills and amendments for a number of reasons, and sometimes they vote with little or no understanding of the bill. A congressman might even arrive at the door simply to vote and be told at the door how to vote. He may know nothing of the bill. He uses his electronic voting card, votes, and then leaves. He may not even know the name of the bill or what it does. Here are other reasons for bad legislation:

1) "This is a crummy bill, but I'd never be able to explain a 'no' vote to my constituents."
2) "I see my entire state delegation is voting no on this amendment. I don't think I want to risk voting yes."
3) "I've just got to vote liberal on this one. My conservative image is getting too hard-core."
4) "This is a veteran's benefit bill? No way to vote no on that."
5) "I don't want to vote that way, but the chairman of the committee will really give me a hard time on that project in my district if I don't support him."

Then there are the "motherhood" bills. They have names like "Youth Camp Safety Act." Congressmen will usually vote for them even if they have hidden provisions that stink.

One of the biggest reasons we get bad legislation out of the House is this: congressmen do not have time to do their job. Does this sound weird? They say it's true. Consider those congressmen who live a considerable distance from Washington. Many travel home almost weekly. While at home, congressmen must be engaged in a constant round of meetings, dinners, etc. They have practically no time to study legislation, and when in Washington, the member usually begins his or her day early, followed by a heavy round of in-office appointments interspersed with the demands of committee and subcommittee attendance. Then when the bells announce the opening of the legislative day on the House floor, things really pick up. There will be numerous trips to the floor for quorum calls and recorded votes on legislation. After the House adjourns for the day, a congressman is usually faced with numerous telephone calls to return and a number of obligatory receptions to attend. Then all of the mail must be read, answered, and signed. Finally, every two years, the congressman must become very actively involved in his re-election. That's why there's so little time.

Now that's the end of the book review. I've only touched on a small portion of the book. There is more—much more—and you need to read it. Here are some further meditations on this book: the Constitution specifically limits the power of Congress and the President. But the Constitution has been ignored. Most of the powers are supposed to be in local government. Congress should be concerned about our defense, our foreign affairs, and to an extent, foreign trade—really, that's about it. But Congress is so much concerned about everything else (which, according to the Constitution, should be managed by local government) that they haven't time to do what they were elected to do. Personally, I believe the most important action that Congress could take is to return to their duties assigned by the Constitution. I believe that Congress should establish phase-out dates for so many of these absurd programs that mostly benefit the bureaucrats—simply phase them out.

In other words, Congress and the President approve the budget that funds these programs every year. If the money is stopped or cut off, the people who feed off the funds will lose interest when their pay stops and find something else to do. But you need to give them a timetable so they can find employment. I know that is an oversimplification, but we must get back to good government. History has repeated itself so many times. Anytime we abandon the Constitution in this country, we get into trouble. It's time again to return to the principles of that marvelous document.

So get a copy of the book *Can You Afford This House,* read it, and then write your representatives. Tell them in no uncertain terms what you think.

Good Ol' Days Produced Funny Ailments

Good grief—in the good ol' days, folks were realistic. When they assigned a name to something, it was descriptive, and you'd readily understand what they meant. Today we've drifted from realism to the unreal. But the old times were real, and a review of some of the terms used to identify diseases will illustrate and substantiate that observation.

When I was a youngster, I was sometimes troubled with "risens." Today, no one has risens—they have boils. Well, not really—they are more apt to have a furuncle or a purulent and painful nodule lodged beneath the skin. Anyway, whatever you want to call it, a risen is an experience you'll not soon forget. After you've had one—and even when another is just beginning to show—you'll know it's gonna be a risen. But I've got to digress here a minute and say something about the old-time treatment of risens. You couldn't do much about a risen until the core was about ready to come out. At that time, Mom would take some flaxseed meal, put it in a cup, and pour hot water over it so's to make a blob. When the warm blob was ready, she'd dab it there on the risen and then take a piece of an old worn but clean bedsheet, fold it up, and put it on top of the blob. Then she'd tear a strip off the sheet to use as a bandage. After a day or so, peel off that bandage, and if the risen was ready, the core would come out, as would all the adjacent hair. A flaxseed poultice worked.

Now, if you were lucky enough not to have risens, you still might wind up with the consumption. Folks don't have consumption anymore. They have tuberculosis now, and regardless of how you describe it, you'll feel just as bad, and your physical situation will be identical. In other words, your lungs are being consumed by the disease, hence "consumption."

Now this still sounds crazy, but everyone back in the good ol' days knew what a midwife did, and when you were ruptured, you knew that, too. But have you noticed that folks aren't ruptured anymore? They have hernias. Well, surely you've been around folks who run off at the mouth, and it would be your pleasure for them to come down with the lockjaw. Sometimes I've thought if anyone had to have lockjaw, either Howard Cosell or Cassius Clay (Ali) would be good choices. But I wouldn't wish tetanus on anyone—even those guys. Now from an old family medical advisor written in 1870, here are some health problems that concerned folks in those times—and some of these problems persist today.

Take whooping cough—well, maybe you don't want to take it, but consider it. The name whooping cough is very descriptive. One whoops with the whooping cough. And should you have the croup, you'll certainly croup as you might also drop with the dropsy and turn yellow with the yellow jaundice. If you simply had a case of the morbid appetite, I reckon you wouldn't care much for eating, and with the St. Vitus Dance, you wouldn't feel much like dancing—but even so, you might appear to be dancing.

Well, when you caught the milk leg, military eruption, itching tetter, and the creeping eruption, there's no telling how you would react. But the scald head, red gum, and sore eyes weren't that pleasant, either. Finally, there were occupational diseases back in those days, too. For example, you might somehow get the clergyman's sore throat. I suppose that disease could only be experienced by men of the cloth. But no matter—in the olden days, you either took something, caught it, or came down with it.

Today, some folks say you contact a disease. I reckon that means you came in contact with it. And others say you contract one, meaning you enter into a contract with it. Regardless, whether you take it, catch it, come down with it, contact it, or contract it, risens, consumption, lock jaw, military eruptions, and the St. Vitus Dance ain't no fun. But at least the old-time descriptive nomenclature can bring a smile.

Even Cows Have Personality

I suppose that those who've not been around animals much might not be aware that, like human beings, animals have personalities. But as any cattleman knows, a cow has a personality. Now some of my cows, I love. And some are just kinda there. Some I just flat don't have much use for. But then there is ol' Sarah.

Sarah isn't named for anyone, but she looks like a Sarah cow oughta look. She's a big, ungainly black Brahma with a white face. Her ears are a foot long, and she has black circles around her eyes like she went a little heavy on the mascara. Sarah never fights with any of the cows, and she would never hook another, even if they came between her and a range cube. If all the other cows broke a fence down and there was only one wire left standing, Sarah would stay where she belonged. She's a mannerly cow. All the other cows and the family love Sarah, and we can't wait each spring for Sarah to have her calf, because we want to know if it is another Sarah. So far she's had two heifers, and this year's calf is beautiful.

Well, besides Sarah, there's ol' Black Muley. Ol' Muley is a Brangus—and a good one. She probably weighs around a thousand pounds and is the character of the herd. Like Sarah, ol' Muley never fights with any of the others. But she does have some weird traits. One of them is that when we drive up to the herd in that old pickup, ol' Muley always—unfailingly—does the same thing. She faces the pickup, lays her ears back, rares back, sucks her lungs full of air, and lets go with an absolute blast—one long, loud bawl. That's it. She always does the same thing. She bows her neck, turns sideways, and acts like she's getting ready to fight. Ya walk up and put your arms around her neck, and she just stands there waiting for you to scratch her ears. If you stand there and don't scratch her, she'll remind you by lifting you off the ground with a love butt. That Muley is a character.

Then there's ol' Big Beefmaster. Big Beefmaster is *big*—real big—and if a cow can look oriental, it's ol' Beefmaster. One day I had to haul the cattle from one side of the interstate to the other, and ol' Beefmaster decided she wasn't going to climb aboard the trailer. So I left her in the pen by herself and took the others over to the other side. When I came back, Beefmaster had cleanly jumped over a five-foot fence and was standing out there in a trap, all alone. I walked up to her and finally coaxed her back in the pen, but she wasn't about to get in the trailer. The trailer was backed up to the chutes, and the chute gates were open. I was involved in something else, and in twenty minutes or so, I looked back over toward the trailer, and ol' Beefmaster was standing up there big as life, right in the middle of the trailer, waiting. So I closed the gates and gave her a ride to the other side. She simply had to be certain that was what she wanted to do.

Ol' Beefmaster is graceful. You could be standing in the middle of a dry cornfield on a still day, and she could slip up on you. More than any other cow, ol' Beefmaster likes to have her ears scratched, and anytime I'm out there, here she comes. If you're not looking her way, you'll feel this nudge—she's there, ready to be scratched.

Well, then there's the other kind—Ol' White, for one. If you guessed ol' White was a white cow, you're right. White used to be at the top of the pecking order. Now she is about number four or five. Like human beings, cows have pecking orders. The herd leader eats wherever she wants, whenever she wants it. And everybody else just gives way. Before I sawed them off, ol' White had some long, sharp horns. She learned to use them, and she uses them often for no reason. She's just mean. White's only thing is fighting. But in February, just after she'd had a calf, she made a serious mistake in hooking Big Beefmaster. That fight lasted about thirty minutes with White giving ground every step of the way. Finally, she turned tail, which means she surrendered, and Beefmaster chased her off in the deep water of the Chacon Creek. I was real proud of ol' Beefmaster.

Ol' White is still a pill, but last year, her calf weighed 560 pounds at six months. So White is still out there, but her horns aren't as long as they used to be.

Well, then there's Buffalo, who has zero personality. She looks real dumb, and she is. There's Kung Fu, who holds the world's high jump record, and she doesn't even use the Fosbury Flop. Elephant, like Kung Fu, is also great at the high jump. In the spring every year, we always say, "I don't believe ol' Elephant is bred." The next time you check on the cows, she's got a calf. She does that every year—crazy.

So the next time you drive by a herd, remember that all of those bovines out there are individuals, and they have personalities, just like the rest of us animals.

Making Do

As inflation continues by leaps and bounds, many of us are beginning to wonder how we are going to make it. One way we might make it is by living within our means and making do. That's what we did in the good ol' days. I well remember how it was then for my family.

Well, how about utility costs in those days? Utilities are a big thing now. The federal government is going to designate $57 billion out of the windfall profits tax for an Emergency Assistance Program. And I think that is for one year. The Energy Assistance Program has been almost a total rip-off to the average American. But anyway, back to utilities in the good ol' days—I should imagine we would use maybe 3 gallons of kerosene in a month's time in our two coal oil lamps. And we probably paid as much as $0.12 a gallon for the kerosene. Well at that rate, our utility costs came to $0.36 per month. That was it—total. "Well, what about air conditioning and heating?" Forget it. No electricity, no fan, and no air conditioning—and no central heat, either, and no electrical lights. "No deep freeze or refrigerator?" Nope.

"What about things like insurance?" We didn't have it. We had only one car, and it wasn't worth insuring. There wasn't the need for insurance like there is today. If you had an accident, it was an accident, and you didn't have some lawyer chasin' after you to sue somebody. If you were in an accident and dented a fender, you looked at each other and said, "Happy you weren't hurt," brushed the dust off, and carried on. We had a little insurance on the house, and Dad had life insurance, and that was all—not much cost there.

When it came to food, we grew just about everything we ate. We had our own meat, eggs, vegetables, fruit, butter, milk, and all that good stuff. We generated all the vegetables we could eat and then some in our garden. Even the folks in town had a garden. A small plot can produce and amazing amount of food, and it's fun.

Well, come spring, all the family members would need a new wardrobe, right? Not our family members. I didn't have a new wardrobe until I was a junior or senior in high school, and that consisted of one suit. Mostly we wore what Mom made on a sewing machine or what was handed down. We never made it on the top ten best-dressed list, but we were warm and generally covered. A person can do a lot with a sewing machine. Pants can even be patched on a sewing machine, but darning socks had to be done by hand. I don't suppose there are many who darn socks anymore. I "darn" mine when I can't find them. We saved money by patching up what we had and just by wearing what we had over and over.

We didn't worry about the high cost of doctor bills. We only went when we absolutely needed to. A cold, for example, will take a week or ten days to overcome whether you see a doctor or not. My mom would cure a cold with a warm Vicks flannel cloth. It worked like everything else, and in ten days or so, we'd be well. Mom was our doctor. She tended to all but the serious illnesses.

At school, we didn't eat in the lunchroom. We had our lunch out of a paper sack and ate it out on the grounds. And speaking of eating, it is fashionable to eat out these days. I can never remember even one instance of my parents going to San Antonio to eat out. If we ever ate out, it was out in the field near a baler or a peanut thresher.

Well, I'm certainly not advocating that we put all of the lawyers, doctors, insurance folks, or food stores out of business, but I am saying that there are options. They may not be as convenient as one would like, and it may take a little more work and initiative, but it is possible to live within your means and make do. And if you want to know something else, it's kinda fun. My family still puts up vegetables and fruit, still makes our own sausage, and we all chip in and do our part. It's an activity that brings us all together, and the outcome is pretty rewarding as well.

Stop the Tide

In computing my income this year, I was shocked to learn that Uncle Sam wasn't satisfied with what I thought was a more than generous helping to the cash I take in and asked for even more. So by scraping the absolute bottom of the barrel, we forwarded what little we had remaining for the bureaucrats in Washington to use as they see fit. It hurt. The amount I had to pay extra—over and above what we already paid—required over three months' work as a commissioner. Well, I sent that payment off on Monday.

Tuesday, I was driving up Highway 173 north of Hondo, and we passed three obviously illegal aliens, who were northbound and just barely visible in the cedar across the pasture. I was still smarting from sending in the extra cash and at that time happened to remember reading what Congressman Trent Lott from Mississippi had to say in a recent article about illegal aliens. Mr. Lott said that illegal aliens cost the US from $13 billion to $15 billion annually in welfare payments, unemployment compensation, and displacement of jobs. Also, illegal aliens send from $3 billion to $10 billion annually out of the country, which seriously affects our balance of payments. Tax evasion probably costs another $115 million per year. When you sum all of this up, you and I pay about $2,000 per head per year for every illegal alien who crosses the border. You know what? I wanted to stop those dudes and welcome them into the United States and say, "Have a good time! You're here at my expense. I sent in the $2,000 yesterday; your way has been paid." I wanted to do this but didn't, so you can say that I'm not doing any more than the government is to stop the tidal wave of illegal aliens into America.

Now this may offend some, but my view is that no Americans are being held in this country against their will. Therefore, we are all here because we prefer to be here, and if we prefer life in this country, then we certainly want to preserve what we have. So if we want to preserve what we have, we'd best do something about those things that are not good for America. The illegal alien problem is not good for America. Today there are anywhere between 7 million and 20 million illegal aliens in America as well as 4 million *legal* aliens in America at $2,000 a year per head! And the birthrate for offspring of illegal aliens rages out of control.

Now illegal aliens do considerable damage to our nation. It has been estimated that at least one million illegal aliens hold jobs that pay well, and some three million hold other jobs. That's four million jobs that could employ US citizens. Not long ago, fifty illegal aliens were caught in Chicago and sent home. One hundred fifty American citizens got in line to fill the positions they had occupied. On another front, illegal aliens use readily available false documentation to take advantage of every government program—food stamps, free education, free breakfast and lunch at school, Medicaid, and aid to families with dependent children.

Really, America must do something about this continuing problem—there's no reason to wait any longer. Lott says there may be a million illegal aliens who enter the US every year. If we don't do anything else—if the government doesn't do anything—then you'd best get on with it: find you a weekend job, moonlight, do whatever you can do to earn an additional $2,000. Then you can sponsor an illegal alien, as I just did. Really, the bureaucrats in Washington don't mind dreaming up programs to support Mexico's social problems, and Congress doesn't mind increasing your taxes to support those bureaucratic dreams. But I say, *stop the tide!* It used to flow in and out; now it just mostly flows in and stays!

Up, Up, and Away

Have you ever wondered what it might be like to fly a big jet? Well, here's a very brief description of the way it is from engine start-up to the time you reach cruise altitude.

When the pilot and navigator(s) arrive at the airplane, the preflight inspections will have been completed. If you are transporting cargo, you'll need to walk through the cabin area and check the tie downs—if you are carrying passengers, no problem. Anyway, climb in your seat, which is always on the left side of the plane; adjust the seat to your liking; and get your oxygen mask ready. Some thirty minutes before takeoff, have the co-pilot put the air traffic control clearance on request. At that point, the tower folks will call the clearance in to the air traffic control people so there will not be any delay once the engines are started. Those big engines will burn considerable petrol while waiting for clearance.

Some twenty minutes before scheduled takeoff, begin the before starting engines checklist. That'll take about three minutes or so to complete. When it is completed, go to the starting engines checklist. You can't believe how simple it is to start one of those big jet engines— not much more difficult than starting a lawnmower. There are a number of items to watch for during the start; mainly you want to make certain there isn't a hot start, which means fire. That's easy to check on, and when there is ignition, the EGT (exhaust gas temperature) will start increasing rapidly as will the engine speed, which you will monitor on the tachometer. When the number one engine is running, you'll start numbers two, three, and four and complete the checklist. Then call for the before taxi checklist. Complete it, and the co-pilot will call the control tower for clearance to taxi. They'll provide taxi instructions to the active runway and the altimeter setting.

When the clearance is received, you kinda lean on the throttles a little—not much or you might damage equipment or other aircraft parked nearby. As soon as the big bird starts moving, climb on the binders (brakes) and assure they are working properly. You'll need them. When you've done that, call for the taxi checklist. The co-pilot always reads the checklists. The pilot will assure that he completes every item he is supposed to complete, and the co-pilot will ascertain that the pilot does what he's supposed to do. You will live longer if you do that. So you make a coupla turns to check that the fight instruments are working properly and complete the taxi checklist. At this point, the co-pilot will call the control tower for ATC clearance, and the tower will (hopefully having read it) say, "ATC clears MAC 40640 to the Rhein Main (Germany) Airport via the Wrightston Departure contact New York Center on 301.4-over." Read back the clearance to the tower for confirmation, and when that's done, complete the before takeoff checklist. By that time, you'll be almost to the runway, and the copilot will say, "Tower, MAC 40640's ready for takeoff." "Roger, 40640 cleared for takeoff, winds 240 at six."

Well, kinda roll that ol' bird out there, and when it's lined up on the center stripe, standup the throttles, check that all of the instruments are in the green, and slowly shove the throttles right on up to takeoff rate thrust. Those ol' engines will be converting kerosene to noise and thrust, and you'll be accelerating rapidly. Your right hand will be on the throttles in case a last-second ground abort is necessary, and in no time, you will be at fifty knots. Take your left hand off the nose wheel steering, and put it on the control column. You'll be steering the airplane with your feet—rudder pedal steering. At ten knots before liftoff (about 128 knots), you'll pull back on the control column, and the nose gear will un-stick (come off the ground). Keep applying the backpressure with your left hand, and at about 138 knots, you'll be airborne. When you have a positive indication on the rate of climb indicator and the altimeter, call, "Gear up." The copilot will acknowledge and raise the landing gear handle. When it's up and in the green, call for the flaps to be retracted. When that's complete, lower the nose slightly and accelerate to 250 knots (that will not take long), and you will be climbing at around three thousand or more feet per minute. So you'll follow the Wrightstown instrument departure (which is kinda like following a roadmap), and at ten thousand feet, you can further accelerate to 280 knots. Sometime before getting to thirty thousand feet, you'll switch from using your airspeed indicator to the mach-meter and continue climbing at .70 mach. Long before that time, though, you will have engaged the autopilot, and it will be locked on to the ground station you are using to navigate. The navigation computer will be killing the drift (cross winds) and following the course you have selected to the next station.

HB with one of the smaller prop-driven "birds."

Now you are sitting there, listening to what chatter there is on the radio and also to some mood music on another radio. Your seat will be in the recline position, and you're sipping on a cup of coffee, feet up on the pedestal, watching the sunrise—up, up, and away!

As your altimeter approaches flight level three-five-oh (35,000 feet), you'll begin to level off and accelerate to cruise mach. At cruise, adjust the throttles to maintain cruise speed, and complete the cruise checklist—and that's it. If you are in the jet stream's core, you'll be smoking along at about six hundred-plus knots groundspeed, and at that speed, in about five hours or so, the coast of England will come in view—super-fantastic, marvelous—if everything works like it should.

And that is a little bit like it is to fly one of the big birds.

Early Warhorse Track and Field

I was in high school during World War II, and to say the least, our record in athletics was pretty grim. Probably the most intelligent thing the administration did was drop basketball. That in itself was a moral victory and probably saved ol' Devine High some degree of embarrassment. We probably should have dropped other sports as well. Here's a good reason why.

Along about the time I was a junior, we had just one coach, and he coached everything. He would say, "Well, think we'll field a track team this year—uh, we'll begin workouts tomorrow, and then the next day, we'll enter the Border Olympics down in Laredo. Uh, Briscoe, you're kinda tall and skinny; you can run the 440 and 880, and, uh, Slue (Schott), you can do the 440 also. Now Adams will be the high jumper ..." and on and on he raved. So sure enough, the next day, we worked out, and the following day, we packed our gear and headed for the Olympics—wow. Now my gear consisted of an old, worn-out pair of tennis shoes and some slightly worn swimming trunks. That was it. Slue didn't have the tennis shoes.

So the next day, ol' Slue and I answered the first call for the 440 yard dash. All of these guys from the big schools in San Antone also answered the call. They had tans; they'd been working out for months. They had nice uniforms, too. Slue was a little darker-complected than I, but that was the first time my hide had been exposed to the elements since the summer before, and I looked like the underside of a frog. Anyway, ol' Slue stepped out there on that cinder track *barefooted*, and that's the first thing the starter saw. "Uh, son, ain't you got no shoes?"

"No, sir."

"You mean you're gonna run on this cinder track barefooted?"

"I'm gonna do my best, sir."

"Okay, go to your marks, get set, *bang!*" We were off. I almost spunout with those oversized tennis shoes, and Slue probably had better traction—but anyway, we got underway, and pretty soon Slue and I were covered with heel dust. We got smoked. We were so long getting to the finish line that we held up the next race. Anyway, after crossing the finish line, we collapsed on each other and held on, dead. Four hundred forty yards is a long way to run with a full head of steam and only one day's workout—wow. Anyway, we sat down there on the grass, and ol' Slue had these great chunks of flesh hanging off the bottom of his feet. Cinders are tough on a barefooted man.

Well, after an hour or so of trying to get my health back, they called for the 880-yard run. If you haven't run the 880, don't try; it isn't worth it A person has to be nuts to want to run the 880. I'd rather be a javelin-catcher than run the 880. Anyway, they lined us up there and went through the same starting procedure, and with the shot, we were all off. Those suntanned dudes weren't just trotting, either. They were smoking. And I smoked along with them for a while. They were striding a little under sixty flat for the first quarter, and I was kinda up there with them, and then all of a sudden, someone dropped a piano on my back. My legs went. My wind went, and the first thing you know, I couldn't see. You'd have to line me up with a post to see if I was moving. To say that my groundspeed deteriorated would be a gross understatement. I flat *caved in* and ground to a halt. The 880 is tough on a fella in tennis shoes with a tan like the underside of a purple frog and one day's preparation.

Well, those were dark days in the annals of Warhorse athletic history, and that day closed out my high school track career. I kinda think ol' Slue ended his career there, too—and ya know, I've never been sad about that.

Saw Bossy

For many years back in the Depression and post-Depression era, my family operated a dairy. It wasn't a big-time operation. Reckon we might have milked anywhere from thirty to fifty cows, but what we did milk was all done by hand. And Dad needed all the help he could get, and for that reason, I can't remember when I was so young that I didn't help with the milking. Edna was my first cow, and I can still remember how she looked from down under. The right front faucet was somewhat overgrown and difficult to grip, and the left front was somewhat smaller. The two rear ones were about the proper size for someone with my size grip. Ol' Edna was a kind and gentle cow, and I stayed with her for three or four years, taking time out, though, when she was dry. But along the way, I picked up other responsibilities: more cows. And I soon had to get the calves in when I came home from school in the afternoon, too.

Anyway, milking was never a drag. If things got kinda boring, there was always my brother walking along there in the summertime with no shirt on—great target. Just kinda crank that ol' faucet up, and with the proper amount of pressure and Kentucky windage, you could reach out there about forty feet or so with a healthy stream of milk. Just let him pass on by, and then *wham-o*—let him have it right in the middle of the back. Or if a closer shot was available, the earshot was always a favorite. Just a little milk in the ear never hurt anyone. It might get a little sticky, though, before you came in to take a bath—but no damage done. Then too, there was always a passel of cats hanging around which you could hit with a few streams, so there was plenty to keep you entertained. But entertaining as it might have been, there came those times when milking was no fun at all. Take rainy weather, for example.

The lot would be a quagmire—mud ten inches deep. You'd have to put on rubber boots and drag through the mud day after day until it dried up. It was a real mess. And worse, the ol' cows would drag their tails through the mud, and if it was in the right season (or maybe *wrong* is the right word), the cockleburs would be thick in those tails, making the worst rasp you ever saw. Let them get that tail wound up and come across your shirtless back with it—whew, that'd smart. Anyway, you'd finally get those old bossies milked. Then Mom would process the milk—which consisted mostly of running it though filters—and then bottle it. We sold it in pint and quart milk bottles door to door in Devine. Delivered to your doorstep, a quart would cost a full $0.07. We'd expect you to wash the bottle and put it back on the doorstep, and then when we left the full bottle the next morning, we'd pick up the empty. At the end of the week, we'd also expect that you would leave $0.49 for the seven bottles of milk. Sometimes folks wouldn't leave the $0.49, and we'd have to leave them a note—"Please leave $0.49 in the bottle in the morning." Sometimes that wouldn't work either, and we'd have to knock on the door. "Hello—uh, you owe us $0.98 now. Can you let us have the money?"

"No, sorry—my husband is out of work; maybe we can pay you in another week or so if he can find a job." Sometimes we never did get the $0.49.

Sometimes we didn't get the milk bottle or bottles or the $0.49. Times were tough. Then come spring, and the bloodweeds would start growing down on the creek—tender green shoots coming out. The ol' cows would eat them, and their bodies would take those green bloodweed shoots and convert then to white milk. That was pretty tough on that old cow to make white milk from green shoots, and God certainly helped her. But try as she might, she could never take the terrible taste of bloodweed out of her milk. The customers would always have a few words to say about that—note in the milk bottle—"Milk tastes terrible; what's the matter?"

"Cows are eating bloodweeds."

"Let them eat something else."

We also sold milk and sometimes cream to the Devine Creamery—Mr. Brown's creamery. We sold the milk in bulk in five- and ten-gallon cans. Ol' Mule Schneider would come out there, take two ten-gallon cans of milk—one in each hand—and just set them up there on the back of the creamery truck. Mule had plenty of practice (weightlifting), and he was strong. A lot of other folks were strong, too. A fella had to work in those days.

Well, that's a little of how it used to be in the dairy business in the good ol' days. You could always recognize a fella in the dairy business right off when ya shook hands with him. He'd have that steely grip, and in cocklebur season, check his face for the rasp effect from ol' bossy's tail. He'd usually be reasonably well-fed—all the milk, cream, butter, and cheese he could consume. Of course, he'd have clabber and cottage cheese, too. You'd not want to look for him around town after 4:00 p.m. or before 9:00 a.m., 'cause he'd be out there in the lot or in the barn seven days a week, 365 days a year, year in and year out. Cows, you see—dairy cows—don't recognize holidays or weekends, and they aren't sympathetic to anyone who wants to sleep in or to anyone who might want to clean the shucks and hay out of the car and go see a friend. So there it is in summary form—the life of an old-time dairy farmer.

Milk Cows, Brood Sows, Chickens, and a Garden

Recently I was talking with Thomas Contreras about the good ol' days. Thomas and I have known each other as far back as I can remember. His father was a butcher, and when my family slaughtered an animal, Thomas' father was always there to help. Anyway, thinking about our conversation—times were a little tight in those days, and food—or the lack thereof—was a problem. But many families had ways of coping. Take a cow, for example—a cow is a walking food stamp, and many folks in Devine kept a milch cow,

"Kept what?" A milch cow. A milch cow—just one—when she first comes fresh (has her calf) and is a good cow, could give four or five gallons of milch—milk—per day. You'd milk her twice daily, and she gave the milk. That's the only way to say it. Some gave their milk grudgingly—wouldn't even let it down until the calf nursed for a short spell. But anyway, sooner or later, they let it down and gave. But if things got tight—and they did around Devine in the deep Depression—a family with a milch cow was home free. There would be plenty of fresh sweet milk, cream for coffee, cereal and ice cream, sour milk for biscuits, cottage cheese, clabber, and even cheese. Then there'd be butter, buttermilk, and whey. The whey would go to the chickens and hogs. Now, if ol' Bossy hadn't already done her part, she'd also provide you with one calf per year, and that would be about three hundred pounds of meat. What did she do in her spare time? Well, she'd keep your milk lot mowed, and if it was mowed too closely, you'd put a rope around her horns and lead her off down on Burnt Boot Creek, and then she'd clean up the weeds and grass along Burnt Boot. God was indeed kind when he provided man with a milch cow. You know, there were plenty of milch cows that traversed the Oregon Trail—walked every step of the way. If we ever designate a national animal, it outta be the milch cow.

Besides milch cows, one could also find chickens right here in town (if you look closely, you might even find a few today.) Like ol' Bossy, the chickens could kinda make it on their own. Just turn a few ol' hens and a rooster loose out there in the yard, and they'd first eat the neighbor's garden, and then go to the next neighbor, and so on. Before long, the rooster would learn his purpose, and soon the ol' hens would take to settin'. In short order, the hens would hatch off, and the neighbors would have even more chickens in their garden. The day the biggest chick came of frying size, he'd be fried. And as the next chick's time came, there'd be more good meals. If a number of hens hatched off simultaneously, some might even get to the broiler stage—or beyond that, to the stewing hen stage. But a hen doesn't get too old or tough to not be good table fare in one way or another. And don't forget that the ol' hen provides eggs, too. God was indeed kind when He provided man with chickens.

Well, come on out back of the house, and there'd be this board pen—slightly odorous—and in there would be the ol' brood sow. Unlike chickens and cows, the brood sow had to be kept in a pen. But it really didn't take much to feed a brood sow. You'd have the whey, and then—I shudder to mention this, but—"Uh, Henry, before you leave on that date, don't forget to slop the hogs." You know where the slop generally came from: table scraps. The hogs got what the dogs didn't eat. And they usually fought the chickens for their share, and sometimes to kinda reduce the competition, the hogs would eat the chickens. Pull up some weeds and Johnson Grass roots, and throw them in there—ol' sow would love it. So at the proper time, herd that ol' brood sow over to a visit with the neighbor's boar, and before long, ya know—eight more porkers. And that's a lot of pork. So a family could sell some of the surplus. God, I think, was indeed kind when He provided man with a brood sow. I'm sure He was. Anyway …

Vegetables aren't bad fare—corn, taters, greens, turnips, tomatoes, squash, beans, peas, cantaloupe, lettuce, cabbage, and more. Wow! And it doesn't take much of a large plot to produce more vegetables than the average family can eat in a year. All it takes is a little elbow grease and a small plot—maybe a little water, and again, some of what good ol' Bossy left there in the cow lot—right here in town. Mr. Willie Schott's father usually had the best and earliest garden in town—beautiful.

Well, that sounds great, doesn't it? But good grief, all of that is work, and besides that, it takes time. In these times, no one is gonna keep a milch cow—even if it were legal. Heck, ya have to milk her twice daily and in the evening. It's at 6:00, that's when the news comes on TV—and that's not all. We've lost the expertise. We can't even communicate with animals anymore. Young people, for example, don't know that you say "Huyee" to Bossy, "Sooey" to the porker, and "Shoo" to the chickens. And that's just to get those respective critters to clear out. Neither would they know that "Sook, sook, sook" means "Come here" to Bossy and "Saw" means to be still. And worse, there isn't a young cow that knows what those words mean, either. Nowadays you have to have a pickup horn to get them to come.

If we could teach the youngsters (humans and cows) to communicate again, and if everyone had room enough for a garden, and if we didn't have the ordinance and no EPA, we might make it if times got tough again. In the slack periods, ya can depend on a squirrel or two—real slack, maybe a rabbit or mud cat caught on doughbait. And if it gets that slack, just move your TV on out to the milk shed, turn it face-down, and use it for a brooder. Then you can set the milk cans on top of it. Shoot, with a milch cow, brood sow, chickens, and a garden, you ain't gonna have time to watch TV, anyway. And that could be one of the blessings.

JUNE 12, 1980

The Promised Land

When I study Numbers and Deuteronomy in the Old Testament, it is difficult not to more or less draw a parallel between ancient Israel and present-day America. I suppose that if I were more knowledgeable or informed on biblical matters, I wouldn't even consider it as being a parallel. But to me, there is a close resemblance.

As you know, God promised Canaan to the Israelites, and after some forty years of wandering in the wilderness, they finally arrived on the east bank of the Jordan River, or the plains of Moab. They were preparing the take Canaan by force, as God had directed them to do, and Moses, in one of his final acts, called the Israelites together to remind them of how they should conduct themselves in the Promised Land. "Hear, O Israel: The Lord our God is one Lord. Thou shalt love the Lord thy God with all thine heart, and with all thy soul, and with all thy might." Deut. 6:4. You can kinda see Moses standing up on a high place, spreading the word.

Now I've flown over what was then known as Canaan many times. Although it might have once been considered the land of milk and honey, the Promised Land as a piece of real estate is not so fertile, not so beautiful, and not nearly so marvelous as the worst part of the American desert. Having flown all over the world and seen the typography of other nations, I can tell ya that if there is a land of milk and honey, it's right here in America. Discounting the oil situation, I wouldn't trade Medina County for all the territory from mid-Mediterranean east through India. I know this is absurd, but if we really got to it, I'm not so sure that we (Medina County) couldn't out-produce that part of the world, agriculturally speaking. America really is the land of milk and honey,

Anyway, there are those historians who say that the Anglo-Saxons who settled the eastern seaboard (except Florida) and from whence our system of law and our language came may have been descendants of ancient Israel, or God's chosen people. Basically, it was the Anglo-Saxons who formed America. They won the Revolutionary War. They sent Lewis and Clark west. They made the Louisiana Purchase, and on and on. The Anglo-Saxons also kind of took Texas, made it an autonomous nation, and then joined the US as a state. They took this continent mostly by force, as the Israelites took Canaan. They won the Revolutionary War against hopeless odds. Certainly the early Americans wandered in the wilderness and survived despite great hardship and against great odds. And many in the early beginning of this country talked about manifest destiny—the idea that America's destiny was manifested by God. And from our earliest beginnings, this nation was, as the pledge to the flag says, "One nation, under God." Today I'm not so certain that's the case.

Now back to Moses and his finals words: "Beware that thou forget not the Lord, thy God, in not keeping his commandments, and his judgments, and his statutes, which I command thee this day: Lest when thy herds and thy flocks multiply, and thy silver and thy gold is multiplied, and all that thou has is multiplied: then thine heart be lifted up and thou forget the Lord thy God, which brought thee forth out of the land of Egypt, from the house of bondage; Who led thee through that great and terrible wilderness, wherein were firey serpents and scorpions and drought. Where there was no water; who brought thee forth water out of the rock of flint. And thou sayest in thine heart, 'My power and the might of mine hand hath gotten me this wealth.' But thou shalt remember the Lord thy God; for it is He that giveth thee power to get wealth. And it shall be, if thou do all forget the Lord thy God, and walk after other gods, and serve them and worship them, I testify against you this day that ye shall surely perish. As the nations which the Lord destroyeth before your face, so shall ye perish; because ye would not be obedient unto the voice of the Lord your God." Deut. 11-20.

Today America has its problems like never before and can't seem to cope with even the more simple situations. It seems that America has forgotten the commandments—the statutes—and many believe that the "power and might of our hands have gotten us this wealth."

Twice on successive and recent Sundays, the lid has blown off of a mountain, which in some way or another has touched practically every state in the contiguous forty-eight states. There has been no recent similar geological event. What does that mean—nothing? I don't know. Could be, though, that God—our omnipotent God, whom all of our coins say we trust in—is becoming restless with America and is simply showing us some small examples of His awesome power. The message might be, "Better shape up, America, and don't forget the commandments—the statutes—the source of your wealth, and your love for God." For as Moses said, "As the nations which the Lord destroyeth before your face, so shall ye perish."

Inheritance Tax as Sure as Death

Of all the taxes that are imposed today in America, the most unjust is the inheritance tax. The federal government and states say, "Okay, ol' Dad, so long as you are living, everything is fine. Your estate is yours. But the minute you die, some of your estate is ours. You may have slaved all of your life and paid income tax and state tax and school tax, city, county, and on and on, and carried your tax load and that of others, but the minute you turn up your heels, uh, we've got to have our share. True, we didn't do anything to help you, but even so, we want part of what you are going to leave here on earth." Somehow that kinda turns my stomach upside down. And my response to that is, "Uh, by what right are you dudes going to take my property? Why can't I designate it for whomever I'd like to have it? And doesn't it follow that if you have the right to take it the instant after I die, couldn't you simply take it right now?"

Really, though, there is no need for me to complain about inheritance taxes. Heck, I only have a small farm and a house—no problem. But it's just possible that I might live another thirty years, and thinking back thirty years to 1950 land values, a person could get all the and he wanted for $30 an acre. Today you've got to plunk down maybe forty times that much for an acre of an averaged-sized farm. Buy a small place, and you're talking maybe seventy to eighty times the 1950 prices. Now consider the year 2010: the illegal alien problem still exists; China continues to have problems, so America takes in half her criminals and a good chunk of her unemployed and unskilled. *The energy problem is worse*—inflation, too. Could it be that land prices will be fifty times what they are today? Surely not—maybe only twenty times what they are today. Okay, ten times what they are today: $10,000 an acre? Your little ol' hundred-acre place, in 2010, will be worth $1 million, and here you are in the middle of a horrendous inheritance tax problem with the hundred-acre place out there in the black jacks that you're running eight cows on. Good grief, the bureaucrats are smilin'. So don't say that you may not have an inheritance tax problem confronting you way out there in the future.

HB on the small farm he inherited.

Today—real life—folks around here have had to sell land they've inherited in order to pay the inheritance tax. That is dead wrong. Others have to borrow great sums of money at high interest rates to pay inheritance tax and retain land that has been in their family for generations. That is dead wrong. Sure, I know there are some loopholes in the law, but even with the loopholes, it isn't always possible to avoid paying inheritance tax. As an American citizen, I don't want one cent—or one cent of a tax break—because someone else dies. Some of those families slaved, used good business practices, make sacrifices, and sustained hardship after hardship. Through horrendous effort, they made it. Through blood, sweat, toil, and tears, they made it. But let the senior partner die, and the feds and state step in. "Uh, our bureaucrats need this money. We've got to run the Rural Free Dial-a-Ride. Got to build all of them government housing projects. Must have all of those clinics, energy assistance programs, food stamps, family planning, free lunch and free breakfast programs, and don't forget AMTRAC. Then there's the foreign aid programs; we'll need to help Iran and support the illegal aliens in this country and hire more bureaucrats to hire more bureaucrats to run our programs to support more folks who have found it to their advantage to retire from work and collect from all the programs."

So basically, it's a program of "reward the nonproductive and penalize the productive." It's guaranteed to upset your stomach.

JULY 3, 1980

To Err Is Human

To err is human, they say. But to err and survive is not always possible. Many have lost their lives because of human error. In the Air Force, it used to be pilot error when there was an accident attributed to the poor ol' pilot. And if the accident didn't kill him physically, it'd kill him career-wise. The Air Force is sensitive about losing a C-5 (that costs us taxpayers close to $56 million) because of human error, so a person kinda wants to be careful for a number of reasons.

Anyway, human error—one time, there was this big Navy landing craft that was headed for Hawaii. The ship's navigator plotted his course but applied the variation (difference between true and magnetic north) improperly. Well, everything was smoking along there fine until in the wee hours, when most everyone was asleep, the ol' ship suddenly ground to a catastrophic halt. They ran into an island. Scratch that one LST. The Navy brass was more than a little unhappy about that, and I doubt that the navigator and ship captain were trusted with another ship. Then …

There were these two pilots, both flight examiners—experienced dudes. Years ago, they were en route from California to Hawaii. Hot pilots they were, and approaching the big rock, they started a descent. One problem in those old birds (this was a C-124) was that when you pulled back the throttles to begin your descent, you'd get a loud, gear-warning horn. The horn operated off a microswitch out in the gear-well to advise the pilot that the landing gear was still tucked in the gear-well. So you could just reach up there and push a little button and silence the gear warning horn. But when descending like that, you'll sometimes encounter conflicting air traffic, and the controllers will ask you to level off at an intermediate altitude. After passing the traffic, they'll clear you to descend further. Sometimes you'll be required to perform a series of these step-descents, and it gets a little tiresome to keep reaching up there and silencing the warning horn.

So the dudes decided, "Shoot, we'll just pull the circuit breaker on the gear warning horn, and then we'll not need to silence the warning horn." So that's what they did, and for the rest of their flight, they lost that safety feature. Also there was another nagging problem. In the landing gear handle, there is a bright red light which goes on when the power is reduced and the landing gear is still retracted. So every time they pulled back the power to descend, that doggoned light would come on. Well, shucks—no problem. Just put a Dixie cup over that light, and you won't be bothered with that glaring red light. Now these smooth dudes had no gear warning systems. So after a couple more descents, they were on final approach to ol' runway 08 at Honolulu International Airport. Everything's going great until they pulled the power back for landing, and shortly thereafter, they could hear the *tick-tick-tick* of those ol' prop blades when they started hitting the runway. The landing gear was still safely tucked in the gear well—human error. You know, those pilots became very unpopular with the leadership. As a matter of fact, they wouldn't even let them return to California by airplane. They had to come back by ship. And to my knowledge, no one ever again pulled the circuit breaker on the warning horn or covered the gear handle with a Dixie cup.

Well, those kinds of mistakes are embarrassing, to say the least. But then there are those little accidents that aren't public knowledge that can hurt almost as badly—little things—and in that regard, I've been real mean to myself on many occasions. Not too long back, I was putting some sheet iron on a shed. I hate that job but was almost through; I had put on about fifteen sheets and hadn't hit a finger or thumb, and for me, that's not bad. I came down there to the last sheet and had to drive a nail through three sheets of sheet iron, so I was really applying the pressure to that ol' hammer—coming down hard—and *whew*. I hit my ol' thumb so hard that it popped like a tomato. That smarted.

Then there was this time I was clipping grass alongside our home, got tired of bending over, and stood up. There was this terrible noise, and I went to my knees. You see, I tried to stand up while directly under an iron hose rack. I still carry the scar from that one. Over the years, I've almost backed over myself with a tractor—that isn't easy—cut off most of one toe with an axe, slammed car doors on my fingers, had a yearling drag a roping rope through my hands more than once, stepped on hot coals while barefoot, and no tellin' what else. Sometimes I think that we human beings should start the day with this or a similar prayer: "Dear Lord, thank you for this fine day. Please help me to get through it without disfiguring or killing myself or anyone else through inattention, carelessness, or neglect. Amen."

The Corny Truth

What is now the Tri-County Co-op was formerly Devine Mill and Elevator, and before that, it was simply The Sheller. Way back there, The Sheller was owned and operated by Adams Company, I believe. And at that time, Adams Company was located where Winns is now doing business. It had the memorable slogan, "Everything from a Ratskin to a Ranch." Later, Loggins and Lilly moved into that building, and they also used that slogan.

Anyway, The Sheller came by that name because that was what it did: shelled corn, and plenty of it. In the days I remember, Mr. Thompson, Wesley's father, was the manager, and there was many a wagonload of corn that passed through that machine. At the height of the corn-picking season, one could see wagons lined up along a dirt road that later became Highway 173. They'd be lined up to the west and extend almost down to where Super S is now located. Those coming up in the opposite direction would cross the tracks, and for some reason—because most of the wagons came from that direction, I suppose—they'd turn and go down alongside the tracks way past what is now Brown's Chevrolet. You'd have to wait a while to unload, and that wasn't such a bad deal either, because you could visit with your friends for a while, and also, you might even—when it came lunchtime—get the world's finest hamburger from "Hamburger" Wilkerson. He'd be set up close to the area below Brown's.

Everyone used wagons for a very good reason. No farmer had a truck. Even if a truck was available, it was still best to use a wagon, because that was the machine used when pulling corn in the first place. To get the ol' wagon ready, you'd put on the sideboards that would bring the box up to about two feet in height. That way you could carry a much bigger load. Then you'd hitch up those ol' mules, load up about four hands, and head on out to the field. Next, get the ol' team and wagon lined up in the row, and everyone would pile out of the wagon—two to a side. You wouldn't need a driver going down a cornrow. The mules would have a wire basket placed over their muzzles. You had to have that, or they would pick corn too, and they wouldn't put what they picked in the wagon. So without the baskets, they'd just waste a lot of corn and wouldn't be paying much attention to their business of pulling the wagon.

Well, each hand would take two rows and start pulling corn and throwing it into the wagon. When ready for the wagon to move up, you'd just holler "Giddyup!" and the mules would respond, and when far enough along, "Whoa!" would stop 'em. When the wagon became almost full, you might have to call two or three times on the giddyup before the old team would take off. If you had only two mules hitched up, you'd best not get the wagon too full if you had to climb a sandy hill on the way to town; they couldn't pull it. There would be nothing more frustrating than to have your team balk. One mule would jump forward and the other backward, and then they'd switch that, and the end result was just that: the end. So you didn't want to overload.

Now you can't imagine how important corn was back in those days. Today when most folks think of corn, they think of the grain. But corn had two by-products in those days—cobs and shucks. The Sheller baled the shucks, and shucks made fine cow feed. Nowadays you'd have a hard time finding a bale of shucks. But we fed many a bale. Then there are the cobs. You could back your wagon up there to the cob spout, and in short order, you'd have a load of cobs. It was difficult to get by without a good supply of cobs. First, it wasn't uncommon in those days for each home to have a small building out back with a crescent sawed into the door. Sometimes one could find a box of cobs within. Then too, one of the kids' chores would be to bring in the wood and cobs. That would be for cooking on the ol' wood stove, and if you want to avoid trouble starting a fire, just soak a couple of corncobs in some kerosene and put them in the stove first, and then put the wood on top. Just put a match to those cobs, and they'd burn forever, catching your wood in the process. But when you unloaded those cobs out of the wagon, the chickens, turkeys, and guineas would find them, and there'd always be a few kernels of corn on each cob—they'd spend days there on the cob pile.

If you need a handle for a file or woodrasp, just get a good-sized cob, break the end off, and stick the sharp end of the file or rasp down into the soft middle of the cob. You'd have a good handle. Need a stopper for a jug or bottle? Go to the cob pile, and you'd find the right size—even one for a barrel. It works. You know about corncob pipes, cob fights, and all of those uses. Man, cobs were a necessity. But today, it's hard to find a cob.

Well, you know what uses corn has—tamales, masa, cornmeal, and feed for the horses, mules, chickens, turkeys, cows, and on and on. In earlier years, some used shucks as papers in which they rolled their own cigarettes. So every farm kept a certain amount of corn. You had to have it for all of those reasons. And you put it in the barn—bin—it might have been a barn before, but the minute you put corn in a barn, it became a bin—weird. Anyway, that's a little about corn, cobs, shucks, wagons, teams, and The Sheller in the good ol' days.

True Class

Those who are fairly recent newcomers to Devine may not know that in times past, there were a number of black families living in this area. I would assume that most of those families were descendants of slaves who were brought to the area by early settlers. In my earliest years, some who were much older may have even been slaves.

Now one person in that category was a very old man when I was a youngster—Joe LaBruce. Joe sheared sheep for my father in the early thirties, and I can remember being at the barn with him and listening to him tell me about the old days. He told me that he could remember when there was no Devine and that the only store in this area was out on the Francisco Creek. That would be the Nixville store. Now if you wanted the world's best hominy, you'd go to Joe's wife, Aunt Delia LaBruce. Just take her the corn and a hominy pot there directly behind where Independent Market stands, and she'd do all the rest. She knew how to make hominy, which is certainly, in these times, a lost art. They were probably both slaves in their youth.

Then, over on the George Schott place, lived Uncle Steven Hooks and his wife. Probably Uncle Steve, too, was a slave in his earlier years. When I became old enough to kinda move out and hunt with my brother, we sometimes drifted up Longhollow Slough to Uncle Steve's house. He'd sit there in the shade and tell us about the old times and many a hunting story.

East of Devine lived still another Uncle Steve, and I cannot remember his last name. But I remember him very well. Every Saturday, he'd come riding horseback down the road, headin' to town. We'd run out in the road to greet him, and he always responded in the same manner. Tall, dignified, he sat ramrod straight in the saddle, and he'd always remove a large cowboy hat and bow with a big grin and say, "Howdy, Mistah Henry." He'd stop for a few minutes and talk, and then he'd be off for town. He had a fine saddle and horse.

Over to the northeast of our home lived the County family—a very large family who owned a long, narrow strip of land there in the 'jacks. Sometimes Willie, Arthur, Virdo, and John worked for my father. Also living in that area was Henry Taylor. Henry was a big man, and he had a big son named Johnny. Johnny was born thirty years too soon. He stood about six foot two and weighed maybe 250 pounds. Strong and cat-quick was Johnny Taylor. Joe Vance, Devine's most noteworthy major league baseball player and holder of the world's record in circling the bases, was about the same age as Johnny. I've heard that Johnny could beat Joe in circling the bases. Today, Johnny could have been all-pro—all-everything in pro football. He had the size, strength, and speed. During college, I used to work at Devine Mill and Elevator in the summer, and Johnny was there then. He was good-natured, and when with him, you had to be happy.

Well, so far as I know, there are no descendants of any of those folks around Devine these days. Many of them died here. Some really never knew what it was to be completely free as we think of being free. Like most of us, they were poor. But I remember those Uncle Steves and Joes and ol' Johnny. And I remember how they were. They didn't have any trouble looking you in the eye when they spoke. And there was pride there and honor and dignity. No one ever gave any of those folks anything—no food stamps, no free lunch, no nothing. They made it on their own. When the socialists give even the able-bodied everything for any reason, they rob them of the opportunity of having self-respect, of living with honor, of having pride, and being a useful, productive citizen. A person doesn't have to have an abundance of material things in order to have class. Dignity and honor and self-respect can come in any income situation if folks are given the opportunity. The Uncle Steves I knew had true class.

Da Nang or Wayne, Maine

The airbase at Da Nang, Vietnam is west of the city. When I served there, occasionally some of us would drive through town to the beach, which was east of Da Nang. I hated that ride; therefore, I didn't often take it. Downtown Da Nang was absolutely indescribable—incredible filth, crud, refuse, litter, plastic bottles, weeds, rags, bits, and pieces—terrible. Downtown Asmara, Ethiopia wasn't much better. Some places in Mexico aren't that great, either. And how about America?

A very few years ago, when European man first came to this country, it was clean—beautiful, gorgeous, un-littered. God made it that way. There were no plastics, no aluminum cans, no rubber tires, and no careless citizens to clutter up the countryside. Sure, the Comanche may have been a little careless and left a few buffalo bones lying about, but when the Comanche hitched his (more probably her) travois to the ol' nag and moved to happier hunting grounds before the sun had long settled, there'd be lobos, coyotes, bear, all kinds of cats, and many other varmints to clean up the litter. Everything was natural, meaning it's in the scheme of things that Nature keeps a tidy house. There were deer, buffalo, antelope, elk, wild horses, and other animals to keep the grass and weeds mowed. When an animal died, there was another kind of animal to clean up the mess.

It was that way here until some one hundred years ago. Then came modern man. And look what man has done in slightly more than one hundred years. We've paved this country, fenced it, concreted it, put high-tension lines all over it, built structures of all kinds, punched thousands—millions—of holes in the land, built pipelines under it, and plowed it. All of these things are necessary to support ourselves as we would like to live. But then we constantly litter our countryside; people daily throw sacks and trash on our country roads. Hundreds of times each day, people throw their beer cans, fast food containers, throwaway diapers, and almost anything everywhere. I live one block outside the Devine city limits and often find beer cans thrown by motorists right in my front yard. Others report a different kind of litter—old, useless buildings that dot the landscape. Driving up I-35 to Ft. Worth, pass Waco, and you'll encounter hundreds of old homes, many falling down. The idea is that one never tears down the old homestead, regardless of what little remains or what its condition might be. Let it stand there and rot. And of course, one doesn't need to travel to Waco to see something like that; you can find it pretty close to home.

Still other forms of unsightliness have to do with the lack of pride when maintaining one's property. You'll find that almost anywhere there's rubbish, overgrown weeds and grass, other crud—rusting appliances, car parts and sundry trash—will inevitably appear. We are covering this country with trash quickly. Remember just one hundred years back right here—no bottles, no plastic, no tires, no signs. It was clean—beautiful. What will it look like one hundred years from today? Unless we do something—and quick—it's going to look worse than Da Nang, if that's possible. We're getting there. Look around. Are you proud of your property's appearance? Think the Da Nang bit is what we should shoot for? Da Nang, Texas. Whoa, boy.

On the other hand, there's Wayne, Maine. That is *the* most beautiful community I've ever seen anywhere in this world—no litter, no weeds, no old broken-down buildings—just grass and trees and trim buildings and class. I can't imagine anyone in Wayne, Maine would have anything but a great attitude, optimism, happiness, and *pride*. None can drive through Wayne, Maine and be unhappy. You've gotta say, "Holy Dinah, this place is beautiful!" It's maintained that way by individuals, by the property owners, and by the citizens themselves. And they still have time to make a living, go to school, play softball, wash their cars, go on a picnic, watch Monday night football—all that stuff. Keeping Wayne, Maine looking beautifully maintained and orderly doesn't really take that much time. And you know, it really doesn't take that much money, either. You'd be amazed how little time and effort it would take: just clean *your* area, and I'll clean and maintain *my* area, and it will all stay clean, neat, and trim all year round. Devine and Southeast Medina County can look more like Wayne, Maine. I'll pick up a few cans and bottles. I hope you'll do the same.

Wayne, *si*. Da Nang, no.

Absentminded Congressional Representatives

When I was sworn in to the Air Force, I raised my right hand and repeated an oath: "I do solemnly swear that I will protect and defend the Constitution and the laws of the United States of America, *so help me God!*" And once again, when I took the oath of office as County Commissioner, I swore the same kind of oath—same words: "I will protect, defend, and *uphold* the Constitution of the United States of America." Even a county commissioner must take that oath publicly—an oath to God. Those are heavy words—meaningful words, but easily understood. Now why in the world are all those public oaths necessary? The answer is simple.

The Constitution of the United States of America is one of the most wonderful documents ever written. It was written by some of this world's most intelligent and foresighted human beings who desired to create something that would serve mankind forever. The Constitution was written to protect us from tyranny—oppressive government—under which most of the world's people now live and have lived in so much of the past. We were to be free from all that.

From the beginning, our elected officials were required to repeat a short oath publicly and to God that they would defend and uphold the Constitution. The founding fathers thought that anyone who took a public oath to God would certainly not violate that oath. That was the single most ironclad method of assuring that our government would be composed of people who would uphold and defend the Constitution. With that said, it might be a good time to ask, "How are we doing? Are our congressional representatives defending and upholding the Constitution?"

The Constitutional Index published by *The Review of the News* provides a quarterly summary of how all congressional members voted on issues which are constitutionally related. From this summary, then, one can very quickly scan voting records and determine who among congressional members have good memories and can recall their oath of office. Also, one can identify those with poor memories. In the first quarter of 1980, the House acted on ten issues of constitutional significance: abortion, welfare reform, Martin Luther King holiday, hospital cost containment, Chrysler loan guarantees, nuclear moratorium, most-favored nation status for Red China, preserving our silver stockpile, air bags for automobiles, and the David-Bacon repeal. A local guy you need to know about is Henry B. Gonzalez. Either Henry B. has never read the Constitution or he forgot his oath of office. On all ten issues, Henry B. struck out. He didn't vote with the Constitution—not once. But heck, Henry B. wasn't alone. You probably watched the Democratic convention and heard speak that great patriot from California, Ron Dellums. He has the same problem as Henry B. He forgot the oath or wasn't aware of what the Constitution says. There are literally dozens of others, too, in the House. New York had loads of those dudes in Congress—California, too—also Illinois, Oregon, and New Jersey. These guys have short memories. They serve only two years. Our guy—Ol' Chick Kazen—supported the Constitution four times out of ten. That's not too great, Chick.

How about the Senate? I don't want you to be depressed, but sadly, Arkansas, Connecticut, Florida, Hawaii, Illinois, Kentucky, Maryland, Massachusetts, Michigan, Missouri, Montana, New Jersey, New York, Ohio, Rhode Island, Tennessee, Vermont, Washington, West Virginia, and Wisconsin are each represented by two senators who have forgotten the oath or don't know about specifics in the Constitution. Many other states have one senator like those above, as do we. Our guy in Washington, Ol' Lloyd, has a real poor voting record—period.

Now the fate of America is on the line. That's a true statement. Those folks have shown in their voting records that they cannot be trusted—even after taking a public oath. They are the types who are directing this country to socialism. Everywhere you find socialism, you find extremely high taxes, a heavy burden of national debt, and numerous regulatory agencies. Some say that socialism is the last step before communism. So when one supports those who do not support the Constitution—even after a pubic oath—one puts the fate of this nation in the hands of a person who cannot be trusted and has demonstrated that he or she does not care about your freedom or your child's future. Such a person might agree to give away the Panama Canal and might even place a higher priority on giveaway programs and reelection than a strong defense and a loss of freedom. How do you want to live the rest of your life—like those in Poland, Cuba, and Vietnam, or like we live in America—*free?*

The Constitution assures your freedom from an oppressive government. The Poles would love to have a constitution like ours and representatives who uphold it. We have a constitution, and if we don't elect people who will uphold it, we—like the Poles—will lose our freedom. And that could happen soon.

Pot and 2-4-D

Out on our farm, the habitat must be perfect for weeds—particularly bloodweeds, cockleburs, and sunflowers. They all do wonderfully well there. The closer one gets to the creek, the better the weeds grow. Without some control, by late June, you couldn't walk through that part of the farm. But in early June, the sunflowers are almost mature. One couldn't find more healthy, mature specimens. About that time of the year, I rent a sprayer, buy some 2-4-D, and get to work. Before the spray hits those old plants, they're strong and look the picture of health. But when that chemical hits them, within a very few hours, the leaves begin to sag. The top part of the plant seems to grow through its growth cycle, and in hours, it kinda turns white and curls up. If it were possible to communicate with one of those plants, it would probably be saying, "Like, psychedelic, man—fantastic—wow!" In a day or so, the plant is all hung over—burned out, listless, and dead. Never again will it be the vigorous living thing it once was, and if it could talk, its final words would be something like, "Man, don't get strung out on the 2-4-D."

Now 2-4-D is to sunflowers what pot (marijuana) is to human beings. That is, both chemicals work on living things. The words that follow aren't my words, but words from people who have been treating those caught up in the marijuana craze. That is one kind of expert—people, medically qualified, with years of experience. Another kind of expert is the youngster who will attempt to get his "friend" to try pot, and that "expert" may be a pusher. It will be to his advantage to get the friend strung out. Contrast the expertise of the pusher with that of Dr. Walter X. Lehmann, who has treated and worked with some three thousand young people. Dr. Lehmann has some strong words to say about pot, and youngsters need to know of his experiences: "Its effects are too often subtle and insidious, with long-range damage difficult to calculate." What that really means is that pot will appear to be doing no damage at all. By the time you realize that it is doing damage to your body, it's almost too late. "I used to think that marijuana created only a psychological dependence without physical addiction. But now I am persuaded otherwise. I have seen too many youngsters suffer terrible anxiety, sleeplessness, sweating, lack of appetite, nausea, and the general malaise of withdrawal ... my patient has not regained the sharp edge, that quality of drive, spirit, and capability that once made him a standout. I am not optimistic that he will ever regain it. From what I have seen, there is no question that marijuana wreaks havoc in the body, brain, and psyche that can't be entirely undone .... Right now, millions of our young people are marijuana users who are performing well and are very sure that they are in firm control of themselves. But as they continue using pot, a gradual deterioration will set in for many of them in all phases of their lives. Grades will slip, athletic prowess will diminish, and there will be trouble at home—all of this compounded by an increasing, witless apathy .... With 16 million Americans currently using marijuana, imagine the enormity of the destruction that is taking place in this generation."

Well that's about enough for Dr. Lehmann to get the point across. But he isn't alone in his alarm. In July of 1978 at the International Symposium on Marijuana held in Reims, France, fifty researchers from fourteen countries presented new studies about marijuana's injurious effects on reproduction, lungs, cellular metabolism, and the brain. In March of 1979, the National Institute on Drug Abuse investigators revealed more evidence of marijuana's harmful effects on the reproductive system.

So were I a youngster, I'd want to remember the words and concern by medical experts in making a decision on whether pot was a good idea or not. I'd give more weight to someone who was medically qualified than someone who might be pushing or others who might be users. I'd also remember that pot is usually the beginning. It is mild compared to some, and still it is devastating.

No one needs pot. Those sunflowers didn't need 2-4-D, either. Chemicals can and will destroy plants and animals like 2-4-D and the sunflowers—pot and your brain, your lungs, and your reproductive capability—and *your life.* Dr. Lehmann says that in so many cases, you can't go back—can't turn it around. Damage is permanent if you have gone too far. So the best recommendation is never to begin—not even the first small step—and if one has begun, *quit now.*

I have no personal experience freaking out on any kind of drug, but I have experience in freaking out. I can freak out on sunsets, bluebonnets, the smell of a rose, watching a redbird or hummingbird, a gaggle of geese, or sandhill cranes heading south; a cold, vine-ripened tomato; or a tree-ripened peach. I've got to warn you, though, that all of those things are habit-forming. But when you freak out on those kinds of things, you'll look exactly the opposite of how a sunflower looks after freaking out on 2-4-D. So it's your choice: you can pay through the nose to destroy yourself, or you can pay nothing to see the natural beauty God put here for you to enjoy. So which way is best? Fifty years as a wilted sunflower doesn't seem like a good option to me.

SEPTEMBER 18, 1980

The Hanging Judge

Talk about a wild place! In the Civil War era, Oklahoma was known as Indian Territory. In those days, Indian Territory comprised seventy thousand square miles, and the only authority and permanent residents were some fifty thousand Indians. There was no law and that made operations convenient for those of somewhat questionable character in neighboring states. When things got hot and the law was breathing down your neck, simply slip across the border into Indian Territory, and you'd be free. Before the Civil War, runaway slaves would move in to that free land and become part of its society. Well, as time passed into the 1870s, more white settlers came into the territory—and with those settlers came violence. In 1872, one hundred murders were committed in Indian Territory, and something had to be done. And something was done. Along came Judge Isaac Charles Parker, the hanging judge of Fort Smith, Arkansas.

Parker was a stern, strong-willed individual who accepted the impossible task of cleaning up the Indian Territory. He arrived in Fort Smith in May of 1875 and went to work. In his first session of court, he tried ninety-one cases, of which eighteen were charged with murder. Fifteen were convicted. One of them had murdered a young cowboy to get his boots and saddle. Another clubbed and knifed an old friend to death to get his pocket money, and a third borrowed a Winchester from a friend then used it to kill him. These guys weren't famous outlaws or known gunmen—just plain drifters or losers, and the hanging judge knew what to do with their kind. There were no rehabilitation efforts, suspended sentences, stays of execution, pardons, or wrist slapping.

The first thing Parker did was construct a gallows upon which twelve individuals could be hanged simultaneously. Following his first trial, they hung six men simultaneously. Five thousand folks showed up to watch the public execution. People came by wagon from over fifty miles away to witness this event. Shortly after 9:30 a.m., the executioner spun the trap. Six men died, and the crowd dispersed. Surely some of the five thousand in attendance may have undertaken a swift analysis of their lifestyle and made some abrupt changes. Even if they did, others didn't, and in Judge Parker's twenty-one years as the hanging judge, he sentenced 160 men to the gallows.

Now in order to do that, he had to have authority and power, which he did. Parker was given exclusive jurisdiction and final authority over all crimes committed in Indian Territory. His decisions could not be appealed to any higher court. The only hope a condemned person had was a pardon by the President of the United States. Parker could conduct his trials without regard to precedents established elsewhere by federal law. He also had the authority to hire a small army of deputy marshals—and this he did—some two hundred of them. They patrolled the territory, and some of those dudes may have been worse characters than the ones they brought in. But bring them in they did, and sentence them Judge Parker did. But some of those two hundred or so marshals didn't make it. Sixty-five of them died in the line of duty trying to carry out Parkers' orders of "bring them in dead or alive." Times were tough.

If wounded, a prisoner was permitted to ride in a wagon, chained to its sideboards. The healthy ones walked alongside at gunpoint. Then when a prisoner finally got to Ft. Smith, he faced the hanging judge and a massive gallows made of twelve-inch-thick oak timbers and capable of ending the lives of a dozen convicts at once. Those were tough but *effective* times.

Down on the Farm

Since most folks depend on farm products for food, it might be well for the non-farmer to know something of what it's like to be a farmer. But before I get into this subject, I want to make three points. First, I don't derive my livelihood from farming (fortunately, or with my luck and expertise, we'd be hungry), and secondly, although I spent the first twenty years of my life on a farm, I'm not an experienced farmer. And finally, our family farm is a very small operation, and we really don't farm but simply grow hay crops and forage for cattle. Even so, by the time you plow and plant, maintain the fences, and feed cattle, a person can kinda encounter many of the problems that a real farmer does. And here are some of those problems.

HB's childhood home outside Devine.

If a place is fenced—even a small place like ours—and if you have a highway and creek running through it and a number of cross fences, before long, you'll spend considerable time maintaining fences. On our small farm, there are between four and five miles of fences to maintain. Termites love the inner part of a cedar post, and this fall, there have been worlds of termites; soon there will be plenty of posts to replace. Also, with the winter and summer temperature extremes, posts contract and expand, and the staples will be pushed out. Then the ol' cows love to stick their heads through the fence to get the greener grass, loosening the wires and sagging the fence— more work. Also, birds love to sit on fences—especially after eating mesquite beans and hackberries. And that causes trouble—they plant those seeds right under the fences, and before long, your fence is grown up in brush. So that requires work, too.

Fences also have gates—or in our case, wire gaps. Twice this year, drunks or idiots (or both) have driven through a gap and destroyed it. In both cases, they drove off and forgot to repair them. A few years back, some clown drove off the Interstate and down through the fence out into the field—made a circle and exited through the same hole. Our bull also exited and I suppose challenged an eighteen-wheeler and lost. We had to buy a new bull and fix the fence. Just last week, some nice guy parked his car on the Interstate, went fishing without permission in our tank, and opened a gap—left it open, and every living animal went out on the highway. I was out of town, and a very nice and considerate neighbor put them back in, but traffic was stopped for a while. The fence along the creek is another situation. We've replaced it three times in four years—washed out from flood water. The third time, we abandoned it. And so it is still washed out.

But fences aren't the only problem or by any means the biggest. Insects are also an issue. Three years ago, there were millions of grasshoppers. They ate everything, and last year, they were back again and did considerable damage. This year, there were no grasshoppers— nothing for them to eat. But finally it did rain, and the grass grew, and the butterflies came, and now we have what must be millions of armyworms. They even eat the weeds. And speaking of weeds ...

Sunflowers, blood weeds, and cockleburs do extremely well on our farm. We spray them every year, and we've not done too badly in controlling them, but every now and then, the creek floods, bringing more seed. And worse than that, the dad-gummed cockleburs can lay out there for what seems like years on end and for some reason not germinate. Then—like this fall, after four years of spraying and no burs going to seed—they germinate. So now I must spray again this fall. There are a million grass burs I must do something about, too. Like weeds, the mesquite comes up along the creek and in the grass fields. Every other year or so, you've got to do something about them. And that means work and money.

If battlin' the elements isn't enough, there are the nice folks who come by your place and unload a pickup full of trash—right onto your place or along the road so the wind blows it all over on your land. Earlier this year at another place, some nice folks came along, cut some wires, penned our cattle, and borrowed two yearling heifers. That was in February, and so far, they haven't brought them back. Then sometime back, another guy borrowed a $600 electric pump, and he hasn't brought that back, either.

My family enjoys vegetables, so we have a garden every year. This spring, I spent an entire Saturday getting the garden plowed and planted, and it all came up in good shape—except the tomatoes had to be planted three times. Then the durn cows broke in and ate most of it, and what they didn't take care of, the drought and high winds finished. We finally harvested four small tomatoes.

Now farm folk must also contend with the government. In our case, the government decided to run an Interstate highway through our farm, and they needed about twenty acres. We must maintain an extra mile of fence, carry excessive liability insurance in case a cow gets out and is hit by a motorist, drive around from one side to another, and finally pay an additional 25 percent in taxes every year for those benefits. Also, the government will want part of the farm once I draw my last breath. I really don't understand why they think part of that farm should be theirs. I know they've thought about it. But they really don't want the farm. No one in his right mind would want it. They simply want you to sell it and then send in the money.

Anyway, that's what it's like on a small place. Now a real farmer has real problems, and I haven't said anything about inflation. Go price a one hundred-horsepower tractor and a gallon of diesel, and the next time you are in the hardware store, pick up just a plain old bolt about one inch in diameter and ten inches long. It's gold. You are talking maybe $12 for one bolt. Then there are rains—or worse, no rain—water problems, high winds that blow down ripe crops, plant diseases, hail, seed that doesn't germinate for one reason or another, and don't forget high interest rates and equipment breakdowns. My father and I have been coping with the things I've mentioned for fifty-four years, and I haven't mentioned that terrible four-letter word—*work*. Tonight, when you sit down to a good salad, a baked potato, and a steak, you'll want to give thanks that America still has a few folks who will cope with all of those problems. I suppose the reason they do cope is, like me, they love it. But at times, farming can get downright frustratin'.

I Appreciate Old Things

Everyone has his own kick going, and one kick my wife and I share is that we appreciate old things—talking about furniture, tools, etc. And if you've been antique shopping lately, you'll know that there are many others who also appreciate old things. You don't only need to visit antique stores. Check the classified ads for antique autos, and you'll be amazed at the price of a Model A Ford. And if you own a mint 1956 Chevy, you can fetch a fat price for it.

I suppose it's the dream of everyone who's interested in antiques to someday encounter a bonanza. When we lived in Illinois, we had that experience. On the way from our home to the Air Force base where I worked, there was a huge two-story house. I drove by it every day and appreciated its beauty. We learned that the old house was built by a German doctor in the 1830s. All of the solid oak beams in it were hand-hewn, and it was put together using mortise and tenon and pegs—no nails in it. A nearby barn was constructed in the same fashion. A friend of a friend knew the owner, and one cold, snowy afternoon, my wife, myself, and some friends of ours went to the owner and asked if we might look at the old home. "Sure, go ahead. But there's no furniture in it. You see, about two weeks back, someone brought some trucks in and stole all the furniture. And if you want to see it, better go now, because an Interstate highway is to pass directly over the spot on which it stands, so it will be torn down soon." What a tragedy.

So we went on down to the old house. We looked it over, and out in back was a workshop. We peered through the window, and it looked as if someone had turned the clock back to 1860. One couldn't really see the tools, because in many places, dust was five inches deep. But we wanted to check out that workshop and went back to the lady and asked if we might go in. She replied, "Certainly."

"Well," we asked, "would you be interested in selling some of the tools if we find something we want?"

"You can have it all—it's junk, and I've got to clear all of that stuff out before they tear it down anyway. Haul it away—you can have it."

Tools and implements from the Illinois homestead.

We finally settled on bringing each of three station wagon loads full of items by her home to establish a value, which wasn't much, because really, most of those items have little or no practical value today. For example, there was an old, hand-carved wooden spoon with the name Sarah on it. Anyone familiar with antiques knows that the spoon did not belong to someone named Sarah. Rather, Sarah was the name of the spoon. In the mid 1800s, folks often named their tools, since it was simple to say, "Hand me Sarah." Then an item of fantastic beauty was a solid oak, hand-hewn lard paddle. That article was used to stir the cracklins when rendering lard. The handle on that ol' paddle probably has the most beautiful finish I've ever seen on anything. No shellac, no sandpaper—it was hand-rubbed through years of use. Another unusual item was an old wooden starch box full of buggy screws—some five and six inches long—and another box full of the old copper rivets used in leatherwork. Some of the items were so old that folks nowadays would not even know how they were identified. A froe and froe club are good examples. They were used to make pailings—hog scrapers—handsome wooden mallets and a number of tools that were one-of-a-kind and homemade, and as of yet, I've not found anyone who knows their purpose.

One of the greatest possessions was a huge oak beam taken from the old barn that was six by eight inches by ten feet. It has the mortise and tenon joint and wooden pegs and probably weighs close to two hundred pounds. Today it is as solid as it was in the 1830s when it was cut. It serves as the mantle in our present-day family room.

It is obvious that most of those items have little practical value but are valued as antiques. Many folks admire those kinds of things, so the demand is up, and if you have some old tools, furniture, junk, etc., best check out the antique value before you decide to toss it. Your junk might be someone else's treasure.

Crystal Ball Gazers

As a pilot for over twenty-five years, I've had more than a few experiences with weather. And weather is a very big concern for anyone flying airplanes. But one of the situations a pilot must learn to live with is this business of inaccurate weather forecasting. Personally, I'm very sympathetic to forecasters, because they have a terribly difficult job; trying to forecast the weather isn't easy. I remember one summer morning, we off-loaded a missile down at Cape Canaveral, and we were due to head back to Moses Lake, Washington non-stop. That's a pretty long flight, and I'll never forget the weather briefing: thunderstorms all the way from the Cape to Moses Lake. Thunderstorms are a very real concern to pilots. If there is any way to avoid it, one doesn't want to fly through a thunderstorm. But knowing that at best forecasting is an educated guess, I decided to take off and have a look first-hand. Eleven hours later, we landed at Moses Lake and never saw a thunderstorm. So predicting the weather is tough.

But predicting football results may be even tougher. Because of my avid interest in Southwest Conference football I always get a copy of the *1980 Texas Football* magazine, which makes for very interesting reading a day after the conference race comes to an end. A review of the predictions will lead one to conclude that most predictions aren't worth their salt. For example, the Texas Football staff polled a great number of football writers and broadcasters in Texas and Arkansas to try and predict how the race would end. They assigned numerical values to the voting and arrived at how the season should end. Houston, they said, would be the eventual winner. The Cougars simply had too much talent not to return to the Cotton Bowl. Well, this past Saturday, it was Rice 34, Houston 7. Rice was supposed to have been at the bottom—the cellar-dwellers. But Houston wasn't the only team to fall to Rice—the Aggies did. Arkansas, TCU, and Rice finished the race in a dead tie with Texas at 4 and 4. The ol' Razorbacks were to have been second. Actually, they finished near the bottom and were clobbered by Baylor (42–15). They were very lucky the score was that low. Had the Baylor coach not been such a fine fellow and put in the second and third strings before the end of the third quarter, the final score might have really been horrendous. SMU also laid it on the Razorbacks pretty heavy, and at the season's end, ol' Arkansas was near the bottom.

The team picked to be in the sixth spot—the Baylor Bears— were the eventual champions. And they completed the season with an 8–0 record within the conference. I saw some of the Baylor-Aggie game, and that was an experience. I say *some* of the game, because it was raining so hard for most of the game that you couldn't see anything. The Baylor guys weren't aware that it was raining. Somewhere late in the third quarter, the score stood Baylor 46, Aggies 0. Some 65,000 sodden and saddened Aggie fans looked on, and according to one nearby fan, the Baylor Baptists may have had a special fan in attendance. This fan noted that every time Baylor scored (often), there was a great flash of lightning accompanied by a deafening clap of thunder.

But not all the sportswriters were terrible at forecasting the season. Skip Bayless of *The Dallas Morning News* predicted that Baylor would win the crown. "I'm always wrong when I pick the obvious—A&M, Texas, or Houston. By himself, Mike Singletary (All-American Linebacker) could be enough defense. Most of the defense is back. Remember, you heard it here first—and probably last." Not bad, Skip. More than one fella said that Texas would win the top spot. But Texas was on the wrong side of the score when they played Tech, Baylor, SMU, and A&M. They finished, as did Rice, with a 4 and 4. The predictors also came up with All-Conference selections. The number one quarterback was to have been Mike Mosley of Texas A&M. Mike was replaced as quarterback in mid-season, transferred to the defensive team, and finally just dropped out of sight. Mike Ford, the SMU quarterback, was to have been the total offense leader. Mike lost his starting position mid-season to a freshman. And there were so many of these weird situations. Tech beat Rice, Rice beat Houston, and Houston beat Tech. It appears that parity is about to become a way of life in the conference, and that's good.

Predictions, though, are tough when there is parity. But predictions, as both sportswriters and weathermen know, are tough no matter what.

Crime Doesn't Pay

I suppose there are few human beings who have gone through life without making mistakes or doing anything wrong. Off the top of my head, I can only think of one person who succeeded at perfection. But I've done my share of dumb things, and I'll never forget one of the dumbest. It might be useful for some of the younger folks to know that in the olden days crime didn't pay—as it doesn't now. But anyway, here's the story.

As I've said so many times, one of my favorite places in this ol' world is the black jacks east of Devine. I grew up hunting dove in that area, and by the time I was fifteen or so, I knew that country like the back of my hand. In those days, most of that country was owned by folks who lived elsewhere, and they usually leased that property in large tracts to folks around in this area. In those times, deer hunting wasn't a big thing. Deer leases were almost unheard of, and deer leases in the blackjacks simply didn't exist. There weren't enough deer then in that area to generate much interest. But there were enough to generate my interest, because that was all I knew when it came to deer hunting. But anyway ...

I was about fifteen when an old buddy and I decided one day that come nightfall, we'd crank up our old family car—a 1938 Ford—and kinda sneak on down in the jacks to do a little deer poaching—night hunting. So we did. I can remember that route down there—probably seven or eight miles east of Devine. Most all the way through was private property, as gates were all unlocked in those days. When we finally got to the big pasture where we were going, we kinda cut off this pasture road and drove down across an opening, crossed another road, and then drove up this little hill. We parked the car behind a large blackjack oak tree that had fallen over. When we parked, a full moon was up, and the weather was crystal clear. It was a perfectly still, beautiful night. So I knew where the five blackjack deer hung out, and we took off down a dry creek bed. About three hundred yards later, I climbed up in a small oak tree right along the deer trail. My buddy went on another four hundred yards or so and climbed up in another tree. We were ready. I had my father's ol' double-barreled twelve gauge, and I suppose he had a similar weapon.

Now deep in the blackjacks at night, if you're fifteen years old, you'll soon learn the jacks is sort of a spooky place. First of all, that country has a million owls. Now most folks think of an owl as a bird which hoots—you know, the *"hoot, hoot"* bit. But what you may not know is that every now and then, an ol' owl will give out with a scream that must surely sound something like a panther. That's real upsetting to a fifteen-year-old brain. And besides that, every time a hickory nut or acorn falls when it's still and deathly quiet, it sounds like the entire area is coming unglued as the thing bounces off limbs and finally crashes into the dry leaves on the ground. One doesn't know if the horrendous noise was made by a deer, another human being (usually bad), a panther, or whatever. But one does know that the noise was made by something—and probably something much meaner and more dangerous than a hickory nut. I just knew that whatever it was must have long claws and an evil heart. That owl did not stop screaming. *Whew!*

After an hour or so of listening to the owls and hickory nuts (and by that time, I was more than a little shaky and flaky), the durn car began to start. You could hear it just like it was under the tree. At that point, things really got shaky. My buddy had to pass right under my tree, so it certainly wasn't him—and why would he be starting the car, anyway? Well, I knew I had to do something, and so I did. I almost fell out of the tree, and when I did, my buddy was standing there. "I thought you were going to drive off without me. Who's starting the car, anyway?" Well, we held a short conference and decided to circumnavigate—keeping our distance—back to the car and check things out. We stayed to the heavy timber. In a few minutes, we were in a position to see the car, and crazy as it sounds, there was no one in the car. The starter continued cranking intermittently, but the engine wouldn't start. The sound was that of a 1938 Ford starter—no mistake. Good grief—had it been a short, the starter would have continued cranking.

Well, we stood there in shock for a couple of minutes, and finally, the car engine started, and the car drove off. But our empty car just sat there. That was kind of frightening. And it was still frightening even when we figured it out. You see, someone else had been slowly rolling through those jacks in a 1938 Ford (like ours—just a random coincidence), crossed the road we crossed earlier, and apparently saw our car tracks. This person in a car behind some brush beyond our car stopped to listen and see what they could hear. In those times, it sometimes didn't pay to investigate strange circumstances down in the jacks, and whoever that was didn't investigate very closely.

When that car was out of earshot, we clambered in our ol' machine and cranked it up. With no light, we bugged outta that jackoak country in great haste. I mean, we lit a shuck—and that was it. That was forty years ago, and I haven't been back in that blackjack country on a night deer hunt since. And I plan to maintain that record. I believe the Lord didn't intend for me to break the law and hunt deer at night, and the message came in loud and clear. It was enough to contend with the screech owls and hickory nuts, but when a fella's car mysteriously begins to start, that's too much.

So if any of you young fellas have thoughts about going deep into the sandjacks—or any other place on a deer-poaching exercise—it ain't worth it. Forget it and do something else. Besides having to cope with owls and such, you may have to cope with an irate landowner, a game warden, a judge, or worse—your own conscience.

The Third Element

The Gross National Product of a nation measures that nation's total productive capacity to include goods produced and services rendered. But a third element in productive capacity that separates America from most other nations is the tremendous amount of giving. And I suppose that as we near Christmas, it is appropriate to discuss that essential element of our society.

So if it were possible to accurately measure the goods and services donated by Americans, it would certainly be staggering. Think about it. If it were not for giving, Devine would have no fire department. Because of donations in time, money, and energy, we have a well-trained, dedicated, and responsive fire department. Except for one small truck, the fire department's equipment is not owned by the city, county, or any other political subdivision which belongs to the FD. Now like you and me, those guys all work for a living. At 2:00 a.m. when it is cold and raining and someone's house catches on fire, these firemen turn to and fight the fire. There are no charges, regardless of where the fire is—in the city or out in the country. Those guys are dedicated public servants who help their community. Without giving on their part and ours, there wouldn't be a fire department, which is an essential part of our community.

The same can be said for the EMS, although some of the employees are paid and the equipment is city-owned. EMS operations depend on time donated by those who are involved in the EMS and by private citizens. When there is a cake sale, many local ladies donate their time and energy to make the cakes and get them to the sale. When other similar fundraising events are necessary, donations are the way the system works. One thing that can really help the EMS is for everyone to simply pay for the services rendered. It is incredible that folks use this absolutely essential service when they are in dire need and then not pay for the service. But anyway, the Fire Department and EMS are two prime examples of giving in this community. There are so many, many more.

Two governing boards that sometimes received more than their share of flak are the city council and the school board. And there are dozens of other boards that may not have quite the responsibility and authority as do those boards but nevertheless provide essential management services. And they all have something in common—that is, the members serve free of charge. Many of those positions require a tremendous amount of time and energy. The Chamber of Commerce sponsors many events in this community—Youth Rodeo, Junior Miss Pageant, Fall Festival, Annual Banquet, and others. Each of those events requires serious work by a great many people. When awards are given (and some awards are expensive), all are donated by the folks right here—the Optimists, Lions, Young Farmers, Homemakers, and other active organizations also assist in many ways.

The churches in this community alone are a prime example of giving. If one appraised the real estate values of Devine churches, buildings, grounds, etc., they would probably be valued in excess of a million dollars. Those facilities were made possible by people who gave.

There are Little Leagues, cemetery associations, Band Boosters, Boy and Girl Scout organizations, Extension Service activities, veteran organizations, the library, and many other medical organizations that need our help to fight cancer, heart and lung diseases, drug abuse, and on and on. Then if you really want to get in the money, there are the political activities. Once you contribute to one of those, your mailbox will be filled every day. If you are a National Rifle Association member, they fight our battles for us in Washington, which takes money. If they don't get the operating funds, we could easily lose our constitutional right to bear arms. If a person is interested in the defense of this nation, there's the American Security Council. They work to provide a better defense posture, but their work requires money, too.

The colleges and universities also require outside funds. If there is any institution that never loses touch with me, it is my ol' alma mater, Texas Tech. Often they just send me blank checks. But once I got one already made out for $15. Good grief, there is no end to the duns.

Without the third element of giving, America would be a depressing place. So this giving bit helps to make American lives quality lives. So I'm happy there is a third element. Somehow, I can't imagine that a Russian would give anything for a cause—probably because he doesn't have anything to give and also because he's already given his body, mind, and soul to the communists. I can't imagine that anyone in Vietnam, North Korea, or Cuba could give much, either. So giving is more or less unique to America, and it certainly helps to make our lives more meaningful.

Now here's the final pitch—the Devine School District recently installed material on the track which will make it one of the better high school track facilities in this area. As a taxpayer who has no children or grandchildren attending our schools, I'm 100 percent *for* that project. I suppose one reason I feel that way is that athletics has been one of the biggest things in my life. Also, what is more wholesome than sports? A good facility will certainly inspire and help our youngsters—girls and boys. When I was in school here, we used a grubbing hoe to dig up black dirt, which was supposed to cushion one's fall in the high jump pit. Of course, we didn't jump that high in those days, and we usually survived the fall. But today, good jumpers use the flop technique, and when executed properly, a flopper will come back to earth on the back of his neck. There is no way any reasonably intelligent being is even going to consider flopping onto dug-up black dirt. The same can be said for the pole vault. If one executes the pole vault properly, he'll land on his back. But no one is going to try that from fifteen feet just to land on dirt clods. Proper equipment is needed. The feds aren't going to provide it, and it isn't in the school budget. It comes down to us, then—the third element.

Our kids need $10,000 right now to purchase the equipment for high jumping, pole-vaulting, and all other events. I believe we can reach that goal—with your help. John Watson, Benny Anderson, and Sid Malone are members of a committee to raise the ten grand. Give one of them a call with your third element pledge.

Fishing on the Chacon

When I was a youngster, the ol' Chacon Creek was literally teeming with fish. And one of my father's favorite pastimes was fishing. But he didn't fish like most folks. I can't remember his sitting on the creek bed holding a fishing pole; that wasn't his bag. The way he fished was to use set hooks or trotlines. Usually, my brother and I would seine the more shallow parts of the Chacon for small perch, red horse, and silverside minnows to use for bait. Then about sunset, when we'd finished milking the cows, we'd motor on down to the deep water and put out the lines. I can so well remember those times. You'd walk by a bush on the bank, and a grasshopper would fly on to the water. Then there'd be this horrendous splash as a big bass took his meal. You could do that almost any time of the day—just walk along the bank—grasshoppers and big splashes. Also, down there at just about sunset, those old fish would be swimming up and down, and sometimes it would look like submarines coming down the creek.

There were some bad times on the Chacon, too. On two separate occasions, the cannery in Natalia released nine substances that killed fish for a long way down stream. You couldn't believe the number of fish and the size of some of those ol' fish—huge. There'd be bass at six or eight pounds and catfish up to twenty pounds and more. Dead fish that size don't provide the most pleasant aroma. You couldn't get within two hundred yards of that creek.

The good times are what I remember best. We'd set those lines out in late evening, and then we'd head home, and before going to bed, we'd return, take the fish off the lines, reset them, and then go back in the morning to take off the fish again and reset the lines. We usually didn't set out a great many lines—but even so, at times, the take would be staggering. I can remember one morning we harvested seventy-five pounds of fish. We had one cat at probably eighteen pounds, a couple at about ten or so, and a great many smaller ones. Sadly, those good times are gone forever, I suppose. That is so for a number of reasons.

One reason is that the fish hatchery closed. It had to be that fish eggs would be released downstream when emptying tanks from the fish hatchery, and our farm was only a mile and a half away. Another situation is that in our area of the creek, where the water was maybe eight to ten feet deep, it is now only about eighteen inches deep. In most places, the creek has completely silted in and probably doesn't average much over ten inches deep. I suppose that has happened gradually as farming up stream and erosion from those farms filled in the deep holes. Another sad affair is that in my youth, there were no carp, and now the only fish one sees of any size are carp. Another factor has been the increased use of pesticides. So the good ol' days of fishing the Chacon are gone—and I suppose gone permanently. Farming will continue, and so will erosion and silt, although many folks are trying to do something about it. But there's no indication the fish hatchery will revive, and the farmers need their pesticides. So the carp situation is a self-imposed problem.

Carp are not native to America. They were imported, like the starlings, the walking catfish, the fire ant, the English sparrow, and the nutria. We could have done well without any of these. But what has happened to the Chacon has happened to streams all over America. So we need to be very careful about how we use our resources or else we will completely sterilize this nation in terms of wildlife and wildlife habitat. Unfortunately, the big question is how we go about it.

We've tried the bureaucratic approach, which is to establish a bureaucracy to control something; the EPA is a good example. If one was able to evaluate EPA's overall performance, you'd probably find that EPA has done more harm than good. Some of the decisions and policies coming from that bureaucracy have been incredible. The use of Mirex to control fire ants is a good example, and there are many others.

So we need to come up with another approach for protecting our natural resources and another way of doing business. Government control isn't the answer.

Brush Country Bull Index

CPSIA information can be obtained at www.ICGtesting.com
Printed in the USA
LVOW061933010612

284316LV00003B/8/P